ONE BIG STORY

BIBLE STORY Coloring & Activity BOOK

B&H KIDS

Nashville, Tennessee

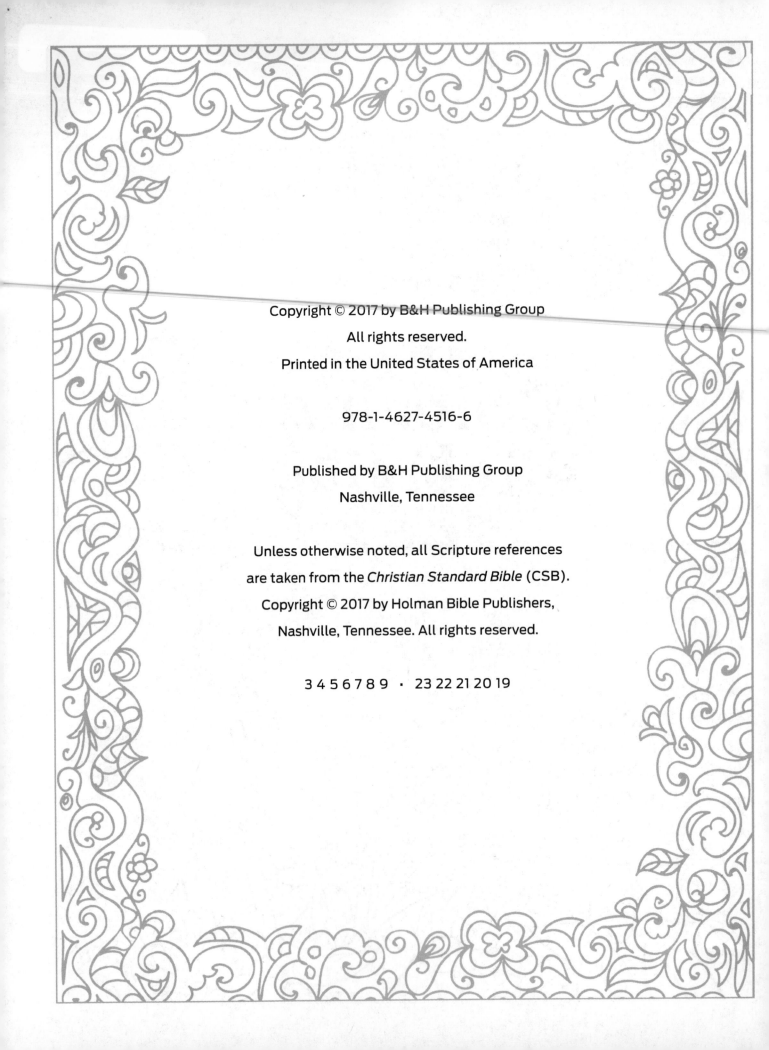

978-1-4627-4516-6

Published by B&H Publishing Group

Nashville, Tennessee

3 4 5 6 7 8 9 · 23 22 21 20 19

A Note to Parents:

A strong foundation in the Word of God is the most important thing you can leave your kids. You want your children to know not only the Bible but also the God who has revealed Himself to us in its pages. The prayer of our hearts is that through the work of the Spirit, God would use His Word to introduce our kids to Jesus. It's a message that we want to give them at home as well as in the church.

All sorts of Bible story products are available today, but they are not all equal. Many Bible products are presented to kids in a way that seems to communicate the primary message: "Be good."

What sometimes gets lost in the journey through the Bible and its many stories is the good news of what Christ has done to save the lost. In other words, when we focus on reinforcing good behavior, we may be missing the heart-change brought about by the gospel. Even worse, we condition our kids to think that the Bible is all about them.

The One Big Story brand has been creating products that focus on the big story, draw our attention to God, and point us to Jesus at every turn. Whether at home or in the church, this *Bible Story Coloring and Activity Book* is designed to serve as both a stand-alone activity book as well as a companion to The One Big Story Bible, Bible storybooks, and devotional.

We understand that sometimes the best way to help a child understand and engage with a story is through physical activity. With coloring pages and activities arranged in biblical order, you can easily find a page that pairs with your current reading and emphasizes key points to remember.

"Be good" is not the message of the Bible. "Be saved" is. We want our children to know that God is good, and He is the hero who sent His Son to die for our sins.

Remember:

For God loved the world in this way: He gave his one and only Son, so that everyone who believes in him will not perish but have eternal life. —John 3:16

Read:

Just before Jesus returned to heaven, He gave His disciples a great commission. This means that He gave all of His followers, even those who live today, a very important job. You can read the great commission in Matthew 28:16–20. Jesus came to save us all from sin. But He also taught us how to live in a way that pleases God. Our very important job is to share everything about Jesus. He wants everyone to know that He came to save us and that God wants us to live a life of obedience to Jesus. Sharing this big news with the whole world may sound scary, but Jesus reminds us, "I am with you always, to the end of the age."

Think:

1. What do all the stories of the Old Testament and the New Testament have in common?

2. The heroes of the Bible often had to be brave for God. What are some ways you can be brave enough to tell others about Him?

3. Name two or three Bible stories that seem to fit together. What did the people in these stories learn?

4. Think of your favorite Bible character. How is your life today different from that person's? How are your lives the same?

5. Jesus came to earth to save His people. Why do you think He came as a tiny baby rather than as a mighty King?

6. If you could write a letter to someone from the Bible, who would it be? What would your letter say?

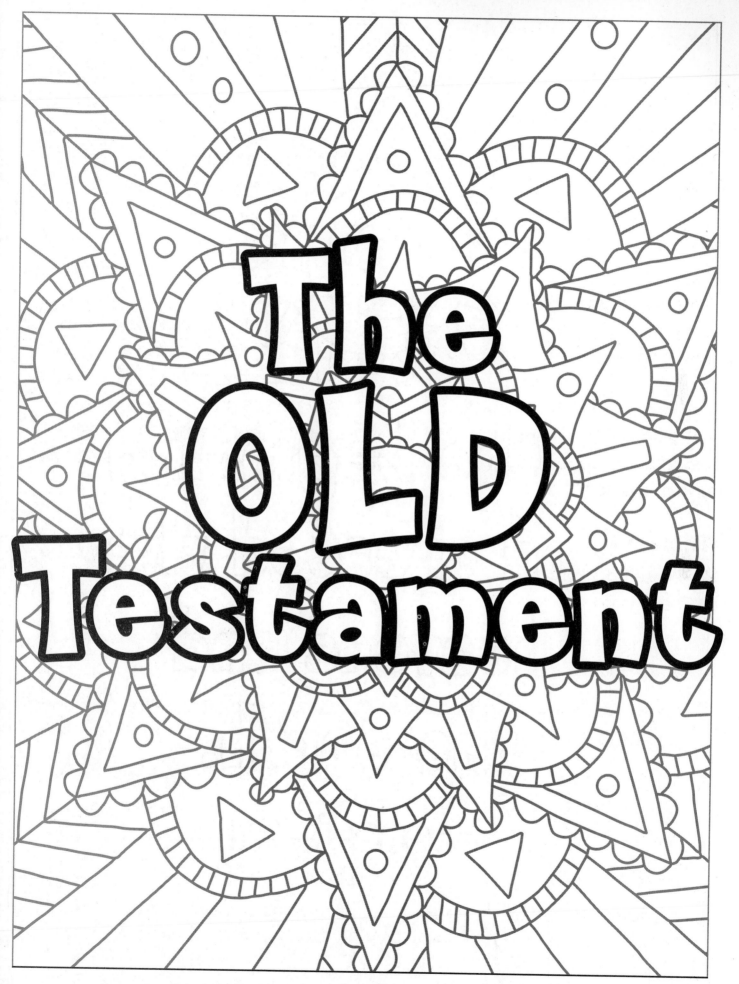

The OLD Testament

In the beginning God created the heavens and the earth.

-Genesis 1:1

Word Search: Creation

Below are some of the things God created in the very beginning. Use a crayon or marker to highlight the words and uncover God's most special creation.

SKY

MOON

STAR

DAY

WATER

PLANT

SUN

TREES

NiGHT

```
A B C A B C A B C A B C A B C
A B C A B C S K Y A B C A B C
A B C A B M O O N A B C A B
A B C A B S T A R A B C A B
A B C A B C D A Y A B C A B C
A B C A B C A W C A B C A B C
A B C A B P L A N T B C A B C
A B C A B C A T C A B C A B C
A B C A B C A E C A B C A B C
A B C A B C A R C A B C A B C
A B C A B C S U N A B C A B C
A B C A B E A B C I B C A B C
A B C A E C A B C A G C A B C
A B C R B C A B C A B H A B C
A B T A B C A B C A B C T B C
A B C A B C A B C A B C A B C
```

Maze: Days of Creation

Find your way through the maze. Start at day 1 and go through all the days of creation to the finish after day 6. What did God create each day?

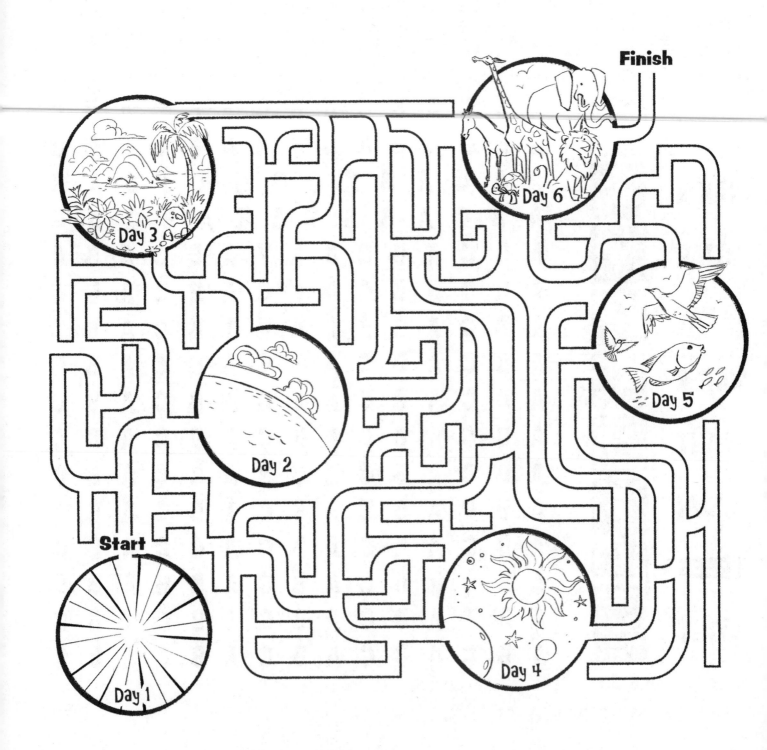

God Created the World

Find It: Hidden Animals

Color spaces with one dot brown. Color spaces with two dots green. Find the animals hidden in the tree and color them any color.

Matching: People of Genesis

Color the pictures of the people from the book of Genesis. Draw lines to match the names of the people with their pictures. Can you find them on other pages in this book?

Joseph

Jacob and Esau

Adam and Eve

Abraham

Noah

God Created People

Cain and Abel

Matching: Cain and Abel's Offerings

God gave instructions to Cain and Abel about their offerings, but only one brother pleased God by obeying. Match the pictures on top with the offerings below. Write Cain and Abel's names on their offering.

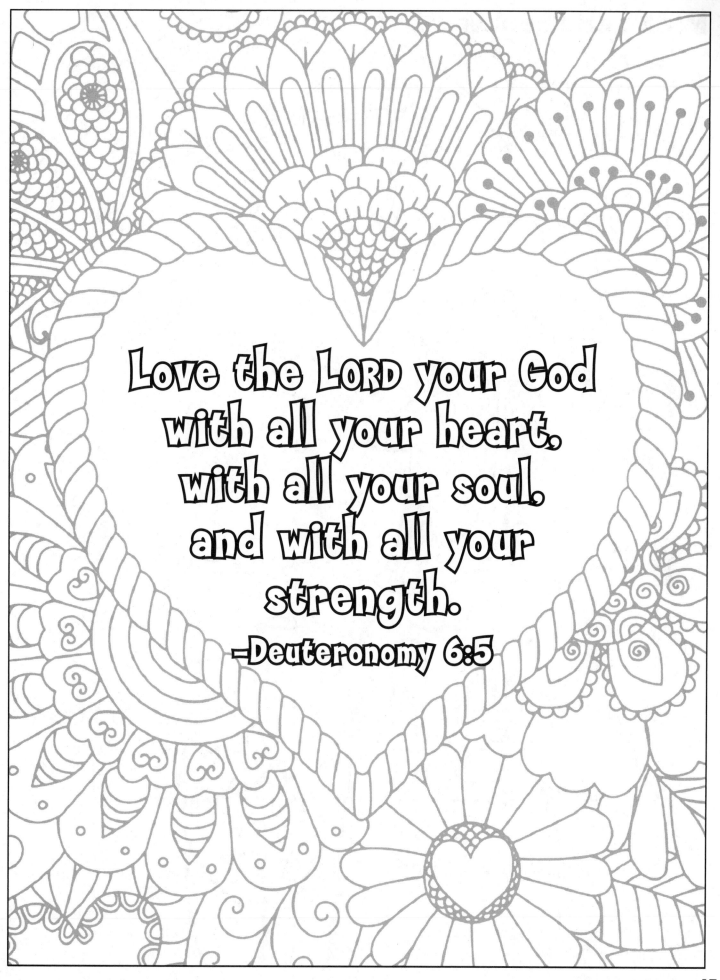

Love the LORD your God with all your heart, with all your soul, and with all your strength.
–Deuteronomy 6:5

Noah and the Ark

God Sent a Rainbow

Find It: Hidden Word

Find the letters for the word "PROMISE" hidden in the picture below.
Color the letters blue.

The Tower of Babel

Secret Code: Brick Tower

Count how many of each letter is in the pyramid and write the numbers in the column to the right. Then place the letter for each number in the blanks on the left to find the name of the tower.

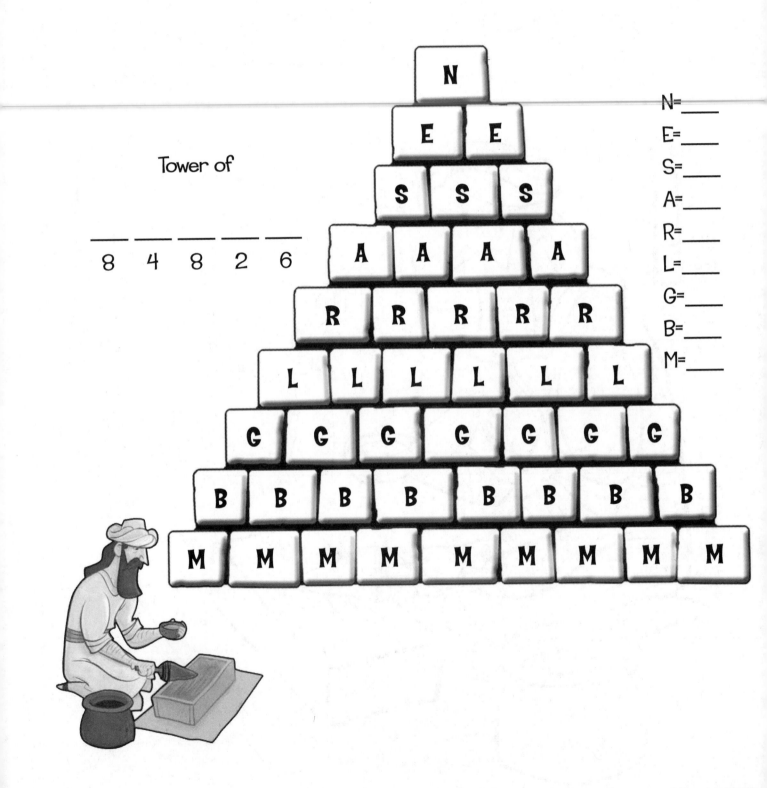

Tower of

__ __ __ __ __
8   4   8   2   6

N=____
E=____
S=____
A=____
R=____
L=____
G=____
B=____
M=____

God's Promise to Abram

Hidden Message: Special Promise

Find out what the special promise God made with Abraham is called. Color the stars that have five points blue. The stars you color will form letters. Place those letters in order on the blanks below. Then color the rest of the stars different colors.

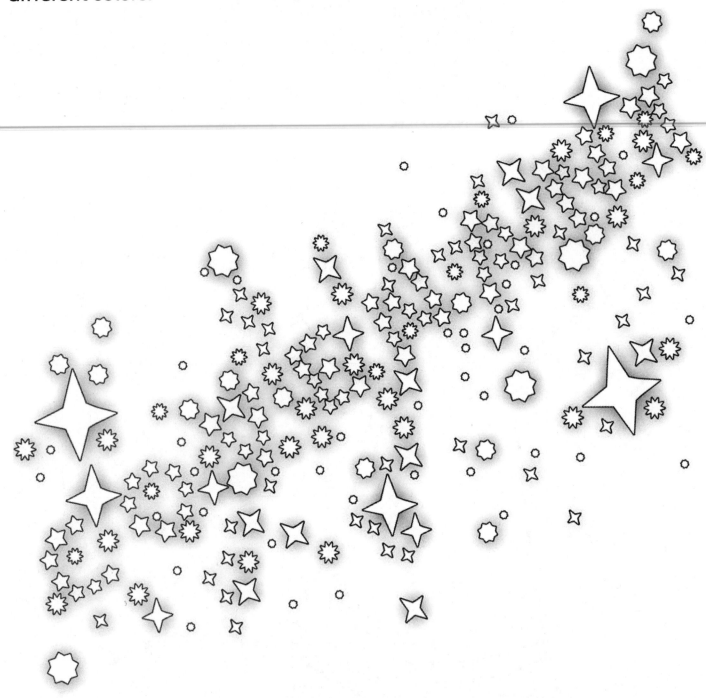

a promise between two people or between a person and God.

The Sons of Abraham

Maze: Amazing Plan

Help Abraham and Sarah get to baby Isaac by finding the right path. Along the correct path are letters that when put together tell us what Abraham and Sarah did when God told them they would have a baby in their old age.

What did Abraham and Sarah do when they were told they would have a baby in their old age?

___ ___ ___ ___ ___ ___ ___

Hidden Message: Abraham

Find the letters in the picture below and color them green to find out what happened when God tested Abraham. Then color the rest of the picture.

The Stolen Blessing

The Promise Reaffirmed

Jacob's New Name

Secret Code: New Name

Jacob received a new name because of something that happened in his life. Decode the sentence below to find out who changed his name and what his name was changed to.

T L W   X S Z M T V W   Q Z X L Y H   M Z N V   G L   R H I Z V O

Example:
T = G

Letter Code

A	B	C	D	E	F	G	H	I	J	K	L	M	N	O	P	Q	R	S	T	U	V	W	X	Y	Z
Z	Y	X	W	V	U	T	S	R	Q	P	O	N	M	L	K	J	I	H	G	F	E	D	C	B	A

Word Search: The Twelve Sons of Jacob

Find and circle the names of all of Jacob's sons.

```
I  C  B  E  N  J  A  M  I  N  K
L  C  M  N  N  L  Z  B  Z  M  W
A  W  N  D  G  E  L  P  Q  V  N
T  J  A  A  B  L  E  V  I  O  I
H  G  K  U  D  M  K  X  E  F  S
P  D  L  N  J  L  M  M  V  F  S
A  U  N  E  A  U  I  Z  W  T  A
N  Z  T  B  Q  S  D  Y  L  Z  C
C  H  D  U  J  H  H  A  X  M  H
Z  H  P  E  S  O  J  E  H  R  A
T  T  P  R  F  L  R  N  R  Z  R
```

1. Reuben	5. Dan	9. Issachar
2. Simeon	6. Naphtali	10. Zebulun
3. Levi	7. Gad	11. Joseph
4. Judah	8. Asher	12. Benjamin

Joseph's Multicolor Coat

Joseph's father gave him a coat of many colors. Color Joseph's coat using as many colors as you can.

Joseph Sent to Egypt

Matching: Joseph Interpreted Dreams

God told Joseph the meaning of many dreams. Match the meaning of the dreams with their pictures and color them in.

A great famine would come to the land of Egypt.

Joseph's brothers would bow down to him one day.

Maze: Joseph's Brothers Traveled to Egypt

Joseph's family were hungry from the famine. They needed to go to Egypt to ask for food. Help Joseph's brothers find their way through the maze to reach Egypt.

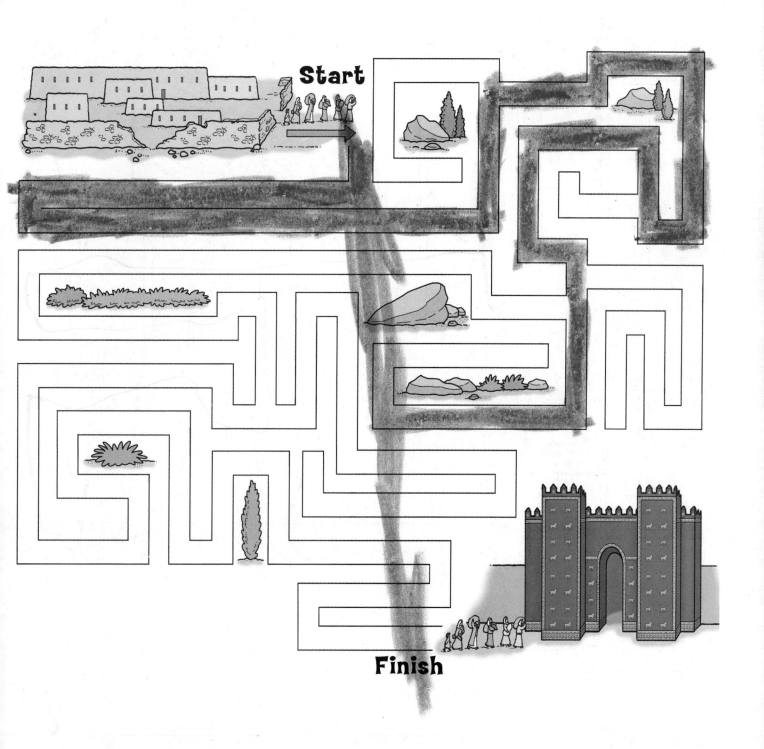

Joseph's Dreams Came True

Genesis 41:53–46:34; 50:15–21

Find It: Hidden Pictures

Find and color the picture of Joseph. Can you find other pictures?

Matching: People of the Exodus and Journey to the Promised Land

Color the pictures of the people. Draw lines to match the names of the people with their pictures. Can you find them on other pages in this book?

Joshua and Caleb

Moses

Pharaoh

Moses Was Born

Color by Number

Color the numbered areas with the colors listed in the key.

1= Dark Blue   4= Brown   7= Light Green
2= Light Blue   5= Black   8= Dark Green
3= Aqua   6= Red   9= Gray

Find It: What Does Not Belong?

Color the picture. Circle the things that do not belong in the picture.

Moses Was Called

Exodus 2:23–25; 3:1–4:20

Maze: Burning Bush

Follow the maze from start to finish.

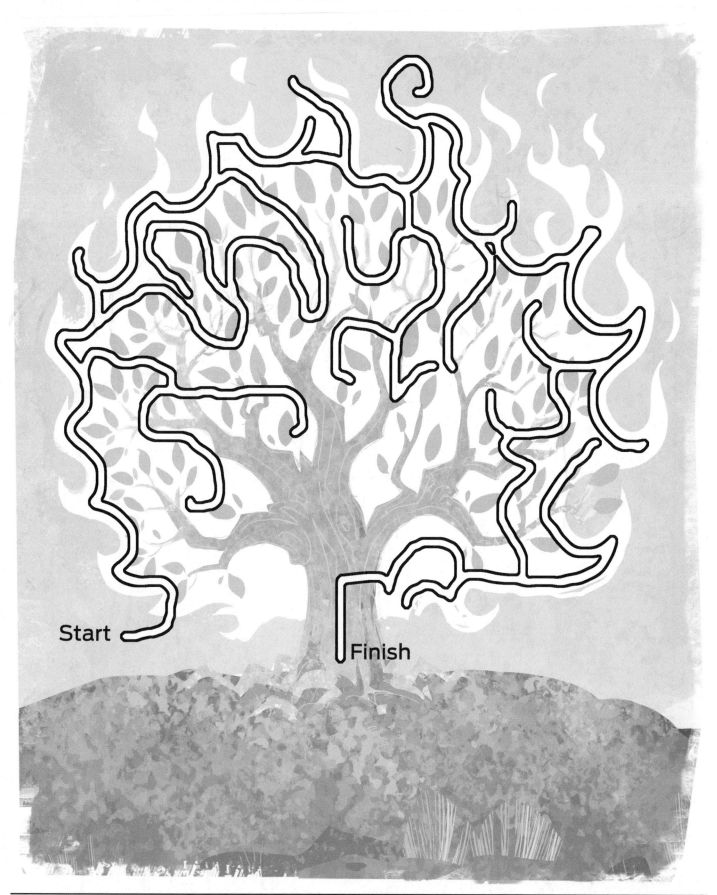

Start

Finish

The Plagues

Exodus 7:14–11:10

What Order?: The Plagues

Put the correct number in each box to put the ten plagues that God sent to Egypt in order.

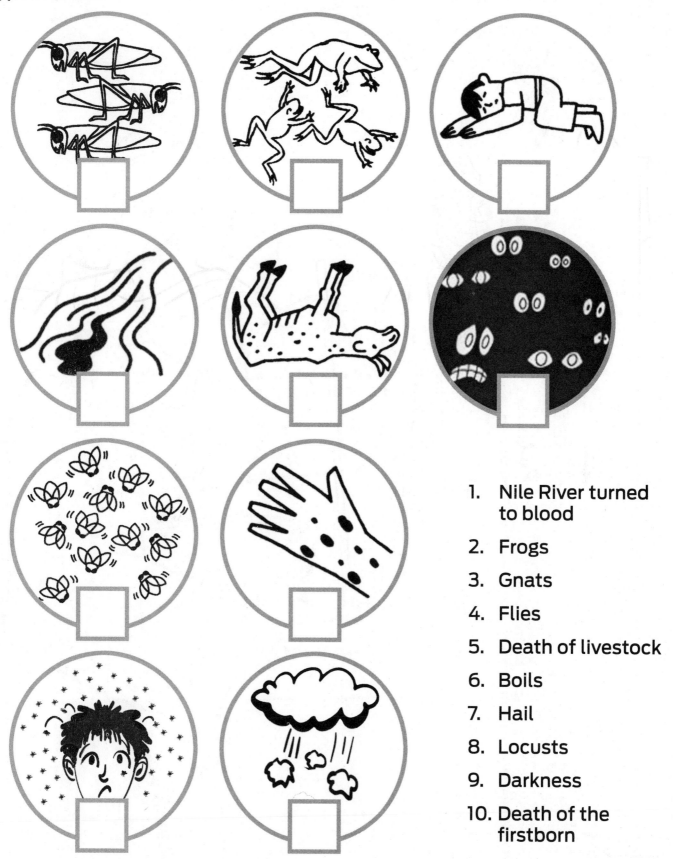

1. Nile River turned to blood
2. Frogs
3. Gnats
4. Flies
5. Death of livestock
6. Boils
7. Hail
8. Locusts
9. Darkness
10. Death of the firstborn

The Passover

Pharaoh Chased the Israelites

The Israelites Crossed
the Red Sea

Matching: Red Sea

Draw lines to connect the fish that match each other.

God Provided Food in the Wilderness

The Ten Commandments

Color by Number

Use the color code to color the spaces and find the hidden word.

1=Blue   2=Red   3=Yellow   4=Orange

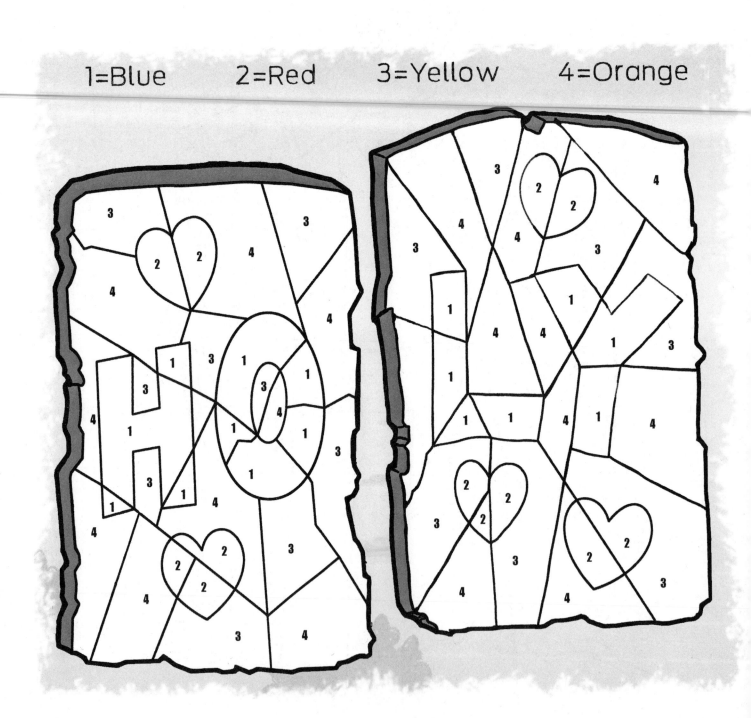

God Spoke from the Mountain

Color by Number

Use the color code to color the spaces and find the hidden word.

1-Yellow   2-Blue   3-Red

The Golden Calf

Secret Code: Moses

Use the pictures to unravel the code. Write the letter for each picture in the blanks.

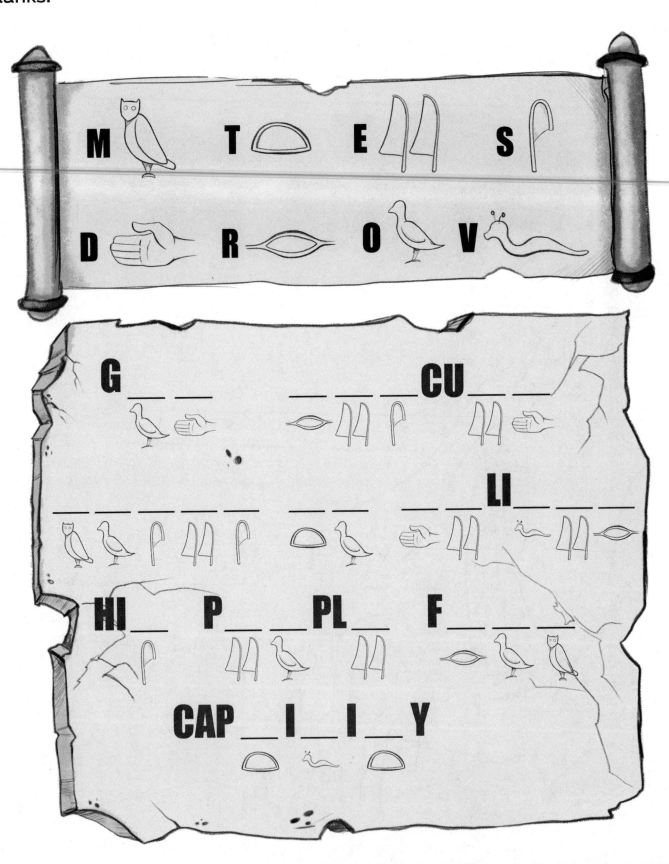

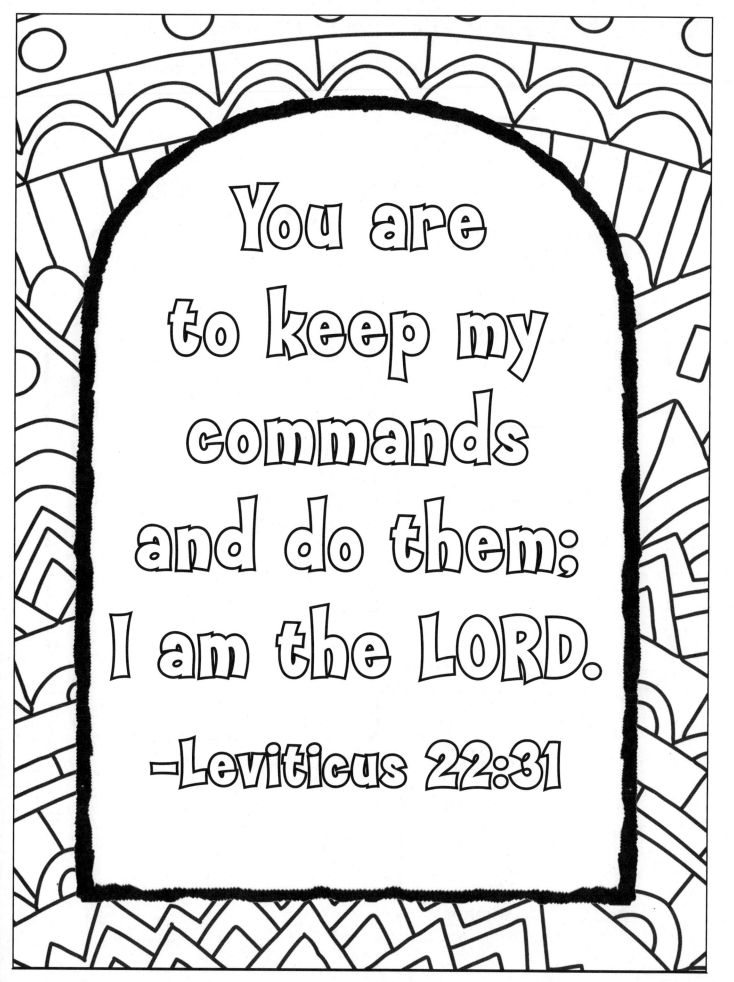

You are
to keep my
commands
and do them;
I am the LORD.

-Leviticus 22:31

Fill in the Blanks: The Ten Commandments

Complete the commandments using words from the word bank.

1. Do not have other _____ before Me.

2. Do not make an _____ for yourself.

3. Do not misuse the name of the _____ your God.

4. Remember the _____ day, to keep it holy.

5. Honor your _____ and your mother.

6. Do not _____.

7. Do not _____ adultery.

8. Do _____ steal.

9. Do not give _____ testimony.

10. Do not covet your _____ house.

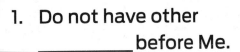

WORD BANK

father	Sabbath
neighbor's	idol
murder	not
false	LORD
gods	commit

Hidden Message: Ark of the Covenant

Color the ark. Find the letters in the ark and color them gold.

Maze: Find the Ark of the Covenant

Complete the maze to help the Israelites find the ark.

Start

Finish

Joshua and Caleb

Maze: Promised Land

Move through the maze to collect each cluster of grapes. Avoid the people already in the land.

Find It: Promised Land

Find the following items in the picture and circle them.

12 spies

1 cluster of grapes

3 trees

2 grasshoppers

1 beehive

The Bronze Snake

Secret Code: Bronze Snake

Use the snake code at the bottom of the page to reveal what the Israelites needed to remember.

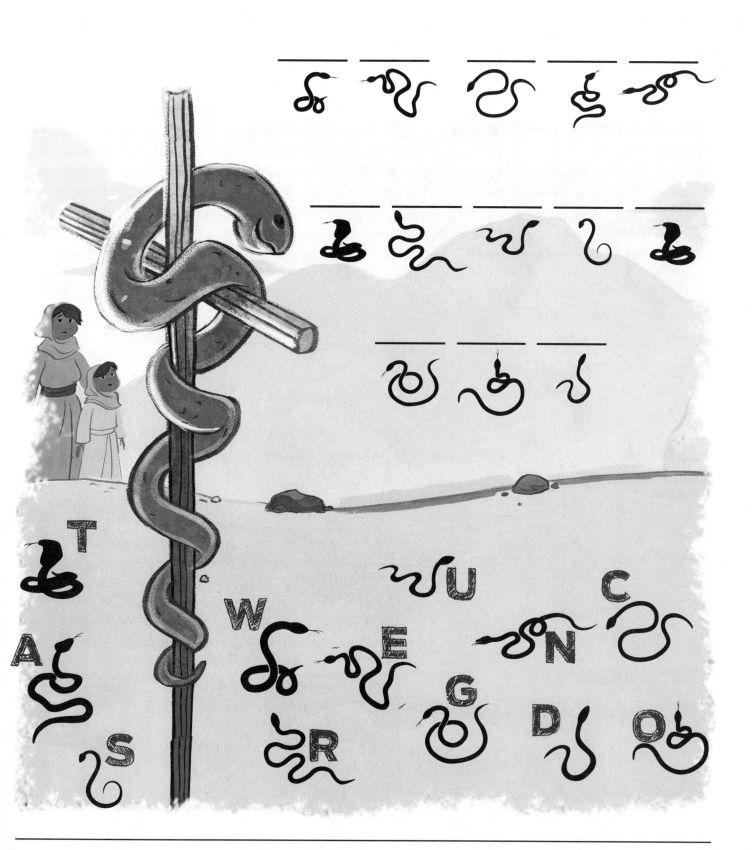

Balaam and the Donkey

Maze: Balaam's Path

Complete the maze to see where Balaam went and whom Balaam saw on his way to King Balak.

The Israelites Crossed the Jordan River

Joshua 1:1; 3–4

Fill in the Blanks: Altar of Twelve Stones

Write the names of the twelve tribes of Israel on the pile of stones. Color each stone a different color.

Asher

Benjamin

Dan

Ephraim

Gad

Issachar

Judah

Manasseh

Naphtali

Reubem

Simeon

Zebulum

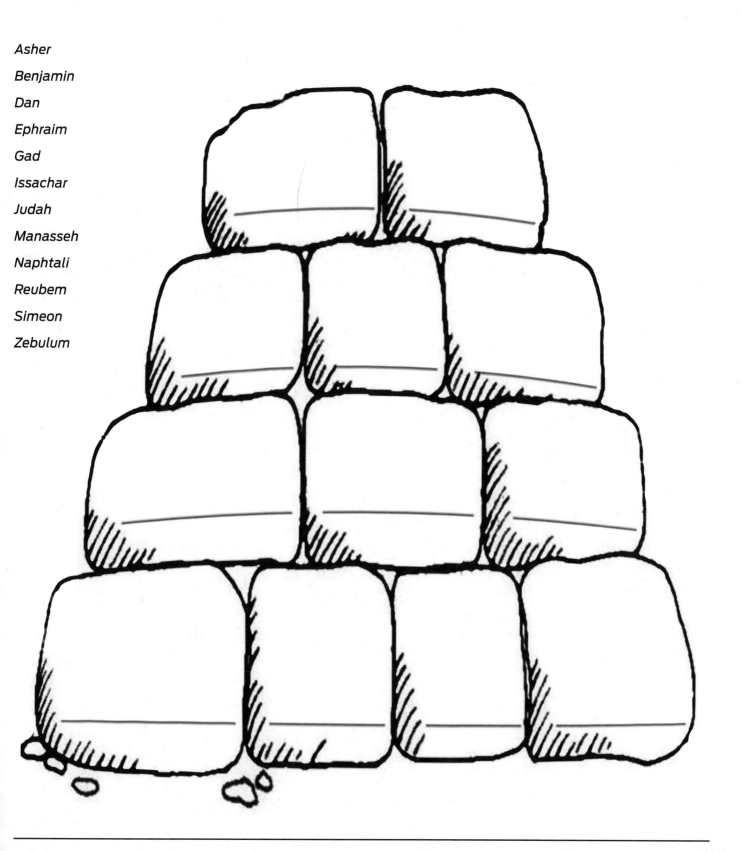

The Tribes of Israel

Color the different tribes of Israel in different colors.

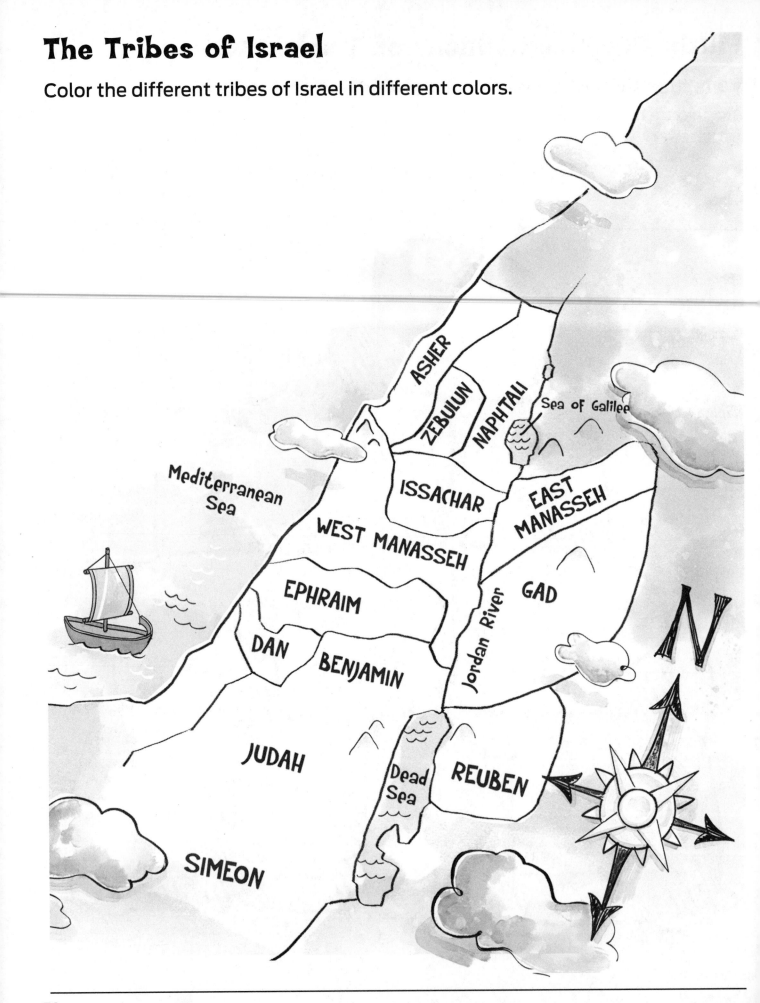

Maze: Promised Land

Complete the maze to help Joshua get to the Promised Land.

The Conquest of Jericho

Word Search: Wall of Jericho

Find the hidden words from the word bank on the wall of Jericho.

```
V  R  H  J  O  S  H  U  A  G  Q  T
J  P  P  S  W  A  Q  O  G  L  X  O
O  O  Y  H  A  Z  Z  G  E  Z  O  V
Q  Z  R  N  L  A  E  R  O  P  E  F
X  N  X  D  L  C  S  T  O  N  E  S
C  B  X  J  A  N  R  H  L  S  G  S
A  T  S  Y  J  N  C  U  E  J  B  L
N  A  O  U  M  I  R  I  T  E  E  D
R  P  T  Z  R  A  P  I  O  R  K  J
J  P  L  E  H  S  R  N  V  Y  Y  V
Z  W  J  W  Z  T  K  C  N  E  Z  M
O  O  N  A  J  S  P  E  H  C  R  G
C  D  F  V  C  J  U  B  Y  U  C  N
Y  R  H  T  T  R  U  M  P  E  T  S
W  B  Y  W  L  R  A  H  A  B  O  H
```

Joshua

Spies

Rahab

Rope

Jordan River

Stones

March

Trumpets

Jericho

Wall

Maze: Jericho

Follow the priests' trumpets to find the way through the maze. Watch out—not all the trumpets are like the priests' trumpets.

Start

Finish

The Defeat of Ai

Joshua Spoke to the People

Secret Code: Remember This!

Decode the message on the stone to find out what the Israelites promised they would do.

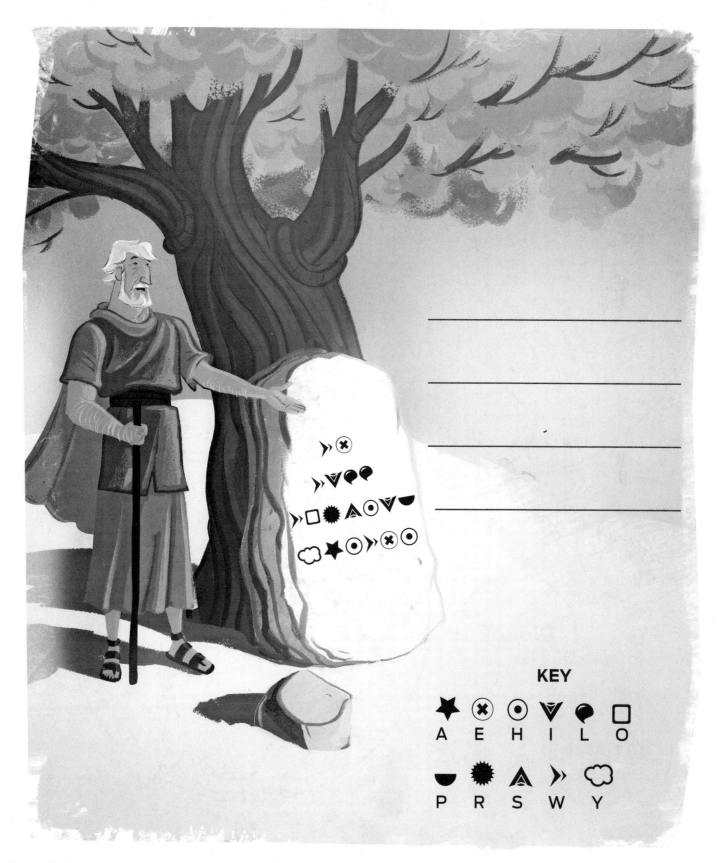

KEY

✦	⊗	⊙	⩒	◗	▢
A	E	H	I	L	O

◡	✺	▲	≫	☁
P	R	S	W	Y

Matching: The People of Judges

Color the pictures of the people from the book of Judges. Then match the names of the people to their pictures. Can you find them on other pages in this book?

Deborah

Gideon

Samson

The First Judges

Find It: What Is Different?

The Israelites began worshiping false gods. Look at the two pictures. Circle the four differences in the bottom picture.

Deborah and Barak

Find It: Who Won the Battle?

Follow the dashed line to see who won the battle. Was it the huge army with 900 scary chariots made of iron, or was it Deborah and Barak's army with no iron chariots? Which army do you think God helped?

Maze: Mount Tabor

Complete the maze to help Barak, Deborah, and the Israelite army get to Mount Tabor.

Gideon

Secret Code: A Name for Gideon

Solve the code to discover how the Angel of the Lord called to Gideon. Each number matches up with a letter of the alphabet. (1 = A, 2 = B, 3 = C, and so on)

1	2	3	4	5	6	7	8	9	10	11	12	13	14	15	16	17	18	19	20	21	22	23	24	25	26
A	B	C	D	E	F	G	H	I	J	K	L	M	N	O	P	Q	R	S	T	U	V	W	X	Y	Z

"The Lord is with you, ___ ___ ___ ___ ___ ___
              13 9   7   8 20 25

___ ___ ___ ___ ___ ___ ___."
23 1 18 18 9 15 18

Samson

Connect the Dots: Samson Was Even Stronger Than This!

Connect the dots to see the mighty animal that Samson killed.

Ruth and Boaz

Unscramble: Gathering Grain

Draw an X on the pieces of grain that have matching words. Then unscramble the rest of the words to fill in the blanks.

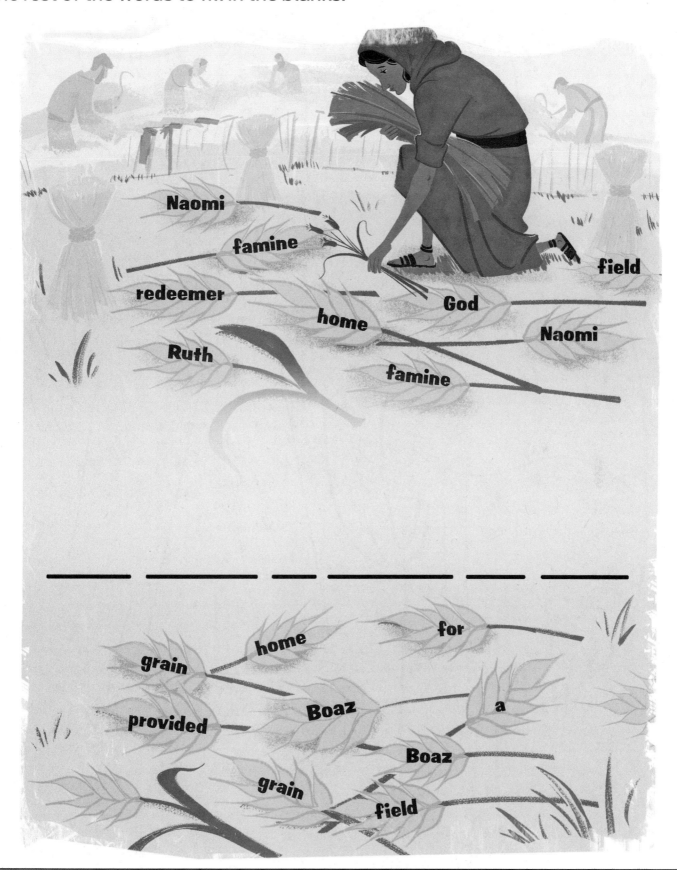

_____ _____ _____ _____ _____ _____ _____

Ruth and Boaz Had a Son

Matching: Kings and Queens of the Old Testament

Color the pictures of the kings and queen of the Old Testament. Then match the names of the people to their pictures. Can you find these people on other pages in this book?

Matching: More Kings of the Old Testament

Color the pictures of the kings of the Old Testament. Then match the names of the people to their pictures. Can you find these people on other pages in this book?

Nebuchadnezzar

evil king

Josiah

David

Eli and Boy Samuel

Hidden Message: Samuel

Color the shapes that are marked with dots blue to see Who spoke to Samuel. Then color the rest of the shapes a different color.

Israel Demanded a King

A Crown for a King

Use markers or crayons to color the crown.

God Rejected Saul as King

Fill in the Blanks: Rejected!

Cross out every third letter to find out what happened to King Saul because he disobeyed God. Write the words in the correct order in the boxes.

G O A D R I E J L E C

S T E M D S O A U K L

A N S K Y I N E G

_____

_____

God   his
of
as   rejected
Saul   king
sin   because

Find It: Who Will Be the Next King?

Draw an X over the pictures that do not lead all the way to the crown.

God Chose David

Samuel looked at all of Jesse's sons before God told him to anoint David to be the next king. Color David and three of his older brothers.

David Fought Goliath

Matching: Find the Giant's Armor

Draw a line from the word at the left to the correct part of the giant's armor. Color David and Goliath.

Spear

Shield

Breastplate

Sword

Helmet

Belt

Shoes

David and Jonathan Became Friends

Partner Games

Find a partner. Play a game of tic-tac-toe. Then play connect-the-dots. Take turns drawing a line between two dots. When you complete a square, write your initials in the square. The player with the most squares wins.

God's Covenant with David

Maze: Ancestors

Make your way through the maze of Old Testament people who are part of Jesus' family. Which Bible people do you encounter?

David Sinned and Was Restored

2 Samuel 11:1–12:14; Psalm 51

Secret Code: Herd Words

Use the sheep code to find out what Nathan told David.

Solomon Asked for Wisdom

1 Kings 2:1–4, 10–12; 3:1–15

The LORD gives wisdom. -Proverbs 2:6

Word Search: Solomon

Find the key words from the word box in the grid below.

```
V H U N D E R S T A N D K U I
B X J N O R P R O V E R B S W
T R U S T S L F G Y C M J O Z
A I A L D D N E T D Z K N C L
F W I U C M L C E D B K S N A
A B T S O L O M O N C T H K N
T J E K U Y V L L D Y C K N D
H F A R I A E T R H W N P I M
E S C V D E C I S I O N S Q E
R W H C W K R U U S B N J W Y
R V I G X I Y Y K M E J O L C
R S N S U N D X T F Y S O R Q
O H G Q E G T B N W O H S P R
```

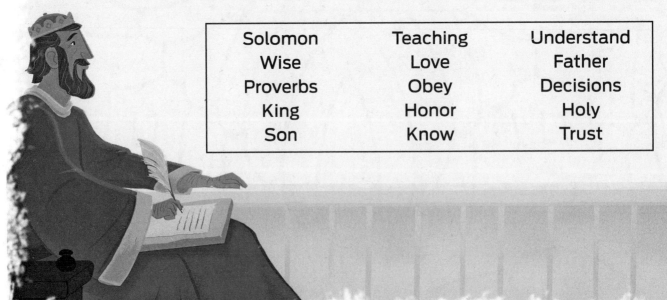

Solomon	Teaching	Understand
Wise	Love	Father
Proverbs	Obey	Decisions
King	Honor	Holy
Son	Know	Trust

Solomon Built the Temple

Unscramble: Temple

Unscramble the letters to find what materials were used to build Solomon's temple. Then draw a line to the picture of that item.

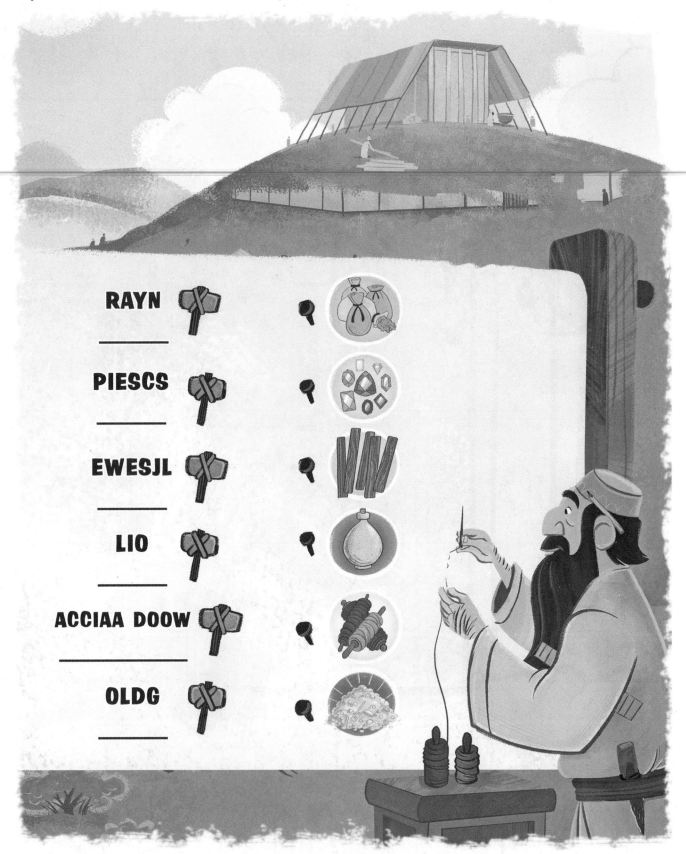

RAYN
_____

PIESCS
_____

EWESJL
_____

LIO
_____

ACCIAA DOOW
_____

OLDG
_____

Connect the Dots: What Did He Build?

Connect the dots in numerical order to complete the picture and learn what Solomon built.

Find It: What Is Different?

Look at the first picture. Circle six things that are different in the second picture.

Find It: What Does Not Belong?

Color the picture of the inside of the temple. Circle the items that do not belong.

Poetry and Wisdom

Secret Code: Music

Each note in the musical code stands for a letter. Solve the code to uncover the secret message.

W__ ___ __N ___U __ __

__O__ __O WO__K __LL

__HIN___ ___ __O__ __OO__.

Find It: Names of God

Find the names of God on the page. Draw circles around those names.

Ava

Noah

Lord

God

Sophia

Ethan

Yahweh

Jacob

Michael

Olivia

Daniel

Emma

Mia

Evil Kings of Israel

Color the Fire

Elijah Ran from Jezebel

Elijah and Naaman

The Northern Kingdom Was Destroyed

Maze: Babylon

The Israelites were exiled to Babylon. Find the way through the maze from the destroyed kingdom to Babylon.

Nehemiah Heard News of Jerusalem

Word Search: News for Nehemiah

Find all the words from the word bank hidden in the grid below.

U F M R J O T R A V E L A N V
U A W E K Q G I O T U G I N Y
X I L A Q B X V J B U P J Y X
S T D Q L B Z L O E C V E Y G
A H O A V L Q J I C R F N N B
D F Q F S A U I U R C N E W S
G U T U N R J J X Z J Z V K P
Q L M L E J B E T L C J T M R
E N K A H A J R D Q F S U Z A
W X I Q E I A U I G O E C U Y
R G N S M W O S U J F H K N B
P Z G T I F D A G Y F A J F S
M M S Y A K Q L L T C N Y E S
V W J T H Z O E C M U A P Z R
J O E O V V S M N Q P K S L I

Nehemiah   wall
news   faithful
cup   sad
king   travel
pray   Jerusalem

Maze: The Way to Jerusalem

Complete the maze to help Nehemiah get to Jerusalem.

Jerusalem's Walls Rebuilt

Matching: Repair the Wall

Draw a line connecting each broken piece with where it goes on the wall.

Maze: Get God's People Home

Complete the maze to get God's people to Jerusalem.

Ezra Read the Law

Fill in the Blanks: Word Wheels

Follow the instructions for each wheel. Use the words you collect to fill in the sentence below.

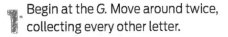
1. Begin at the *G.* Move around twice, collecting every other letter.

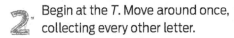
2. Begin at the *T.* Move around once, collecting every other letter.

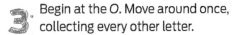
3. Begin at the *O.* Move around once, collecting every other letter.

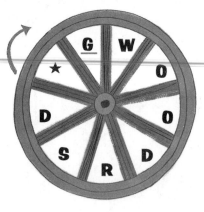
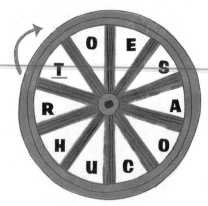
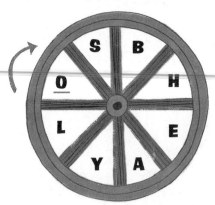

Ezra read __ __ __ ' __   __ __ __ __ __   to   __ __ __ __ __

the people how to __ __ __ __ God.

Esther Became Queen

Secret Code: Esther

Use the code at the bottom to fill in the blanks.

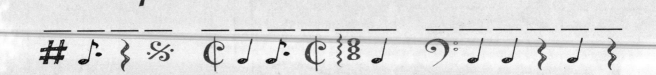

C D E F G H I L M N O P R S T U

Maze: Approach the King

Complete the maze to help Esther arrive in the king's throne room.

Maze: Esther's Quest

Trace the path from Esther to King Ahasuerus.

Finish

Start

Unscramble: Saved from Destruction

Unscramble the mixed-up words. What does this story teach us about Jesus?

God was in control over _____'s evil
(ANMAH)

plan to destroy the _____. Like Haman,
(ESWJ)

_____ wants to destroy believers. Satan
(TSAAN)

thought he had won when _____ died
(EUSSJ)

on the cross, but God raised Jesus from

the _____ and defeated Satan
(DAED)

once and for _____.
(LAL)

God Saved His People Through Esther

This is the day
the LORD has made;
let us rejoice and
be glad in it.
-Psalm 118:24

Job Suffered

Job Worshiped God

Secret Code: The Heavens Declare

Use the key below to match the planets and stars with their letters to figure out the words.

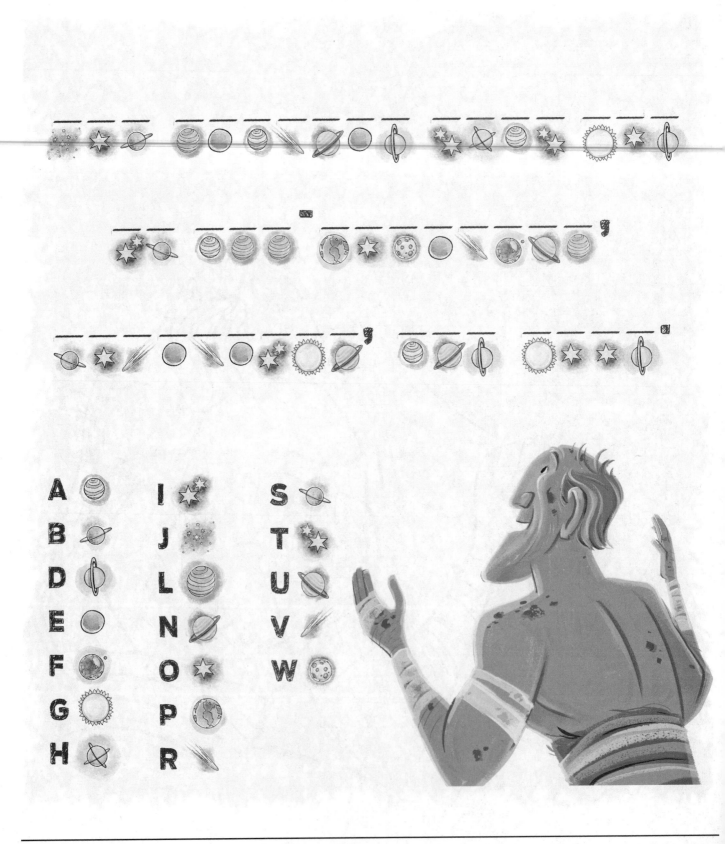

Psalms to Praise God

Matching: Psalms

Draw a line to connect each verse from Psalms with its reference. Color each set the same color.

The LORD is good to everyone; his compassion rests on all he has made.

Psalm 119:11

Psalm 54:2

I have treasured your word in my heart so that I may not sin against you.

God, hear my prayer; listen to the words from my mouth.

Psalm 145:9

Matching: Major Prophets

Color the pictures of the major prophets. Then match the names of the people to their pictures. Can you find them on other pages in this book?

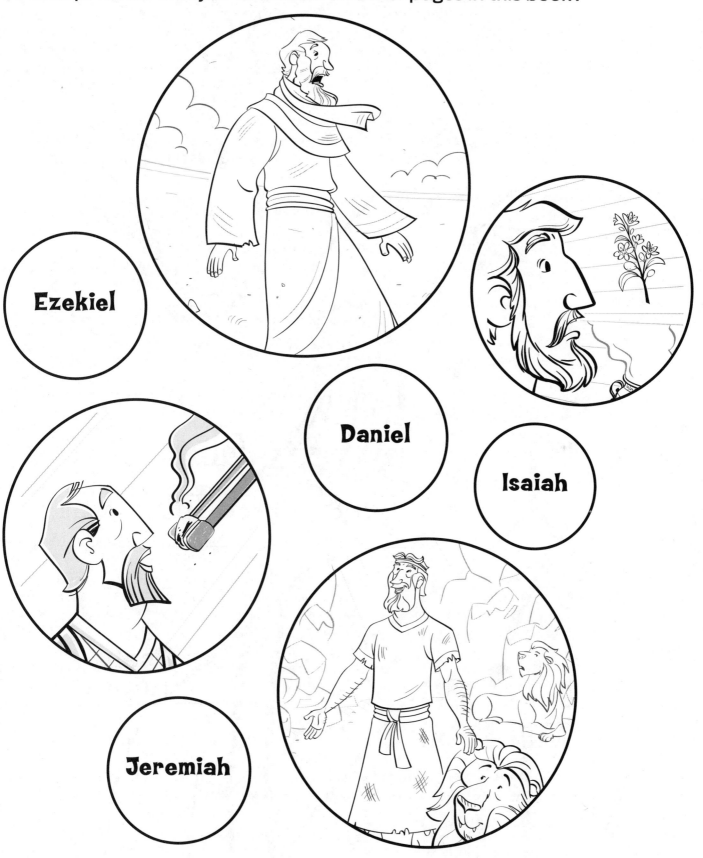

Ezekiel

Daniel

Isaiah

Jeremiah

God Called Isaiah

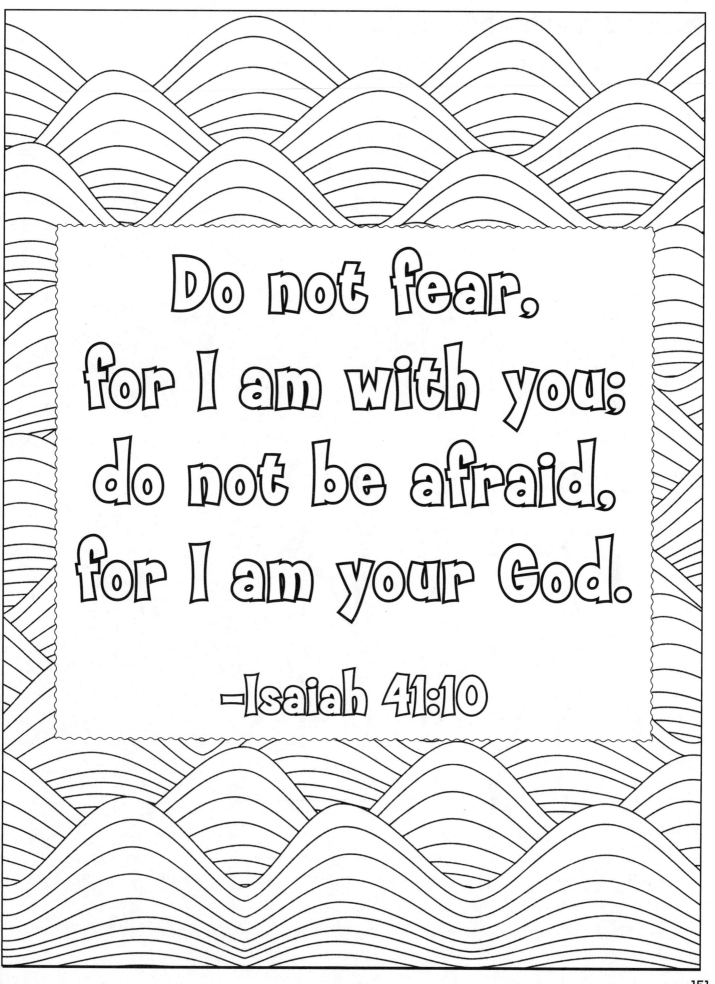

Do not fear, for I am with you; do not be afraid, for I am your God.

-Isaiah 41:10

Word Search: Holy, Holy, Holy

Find and circle the three times the word *holy* appears in the word search.

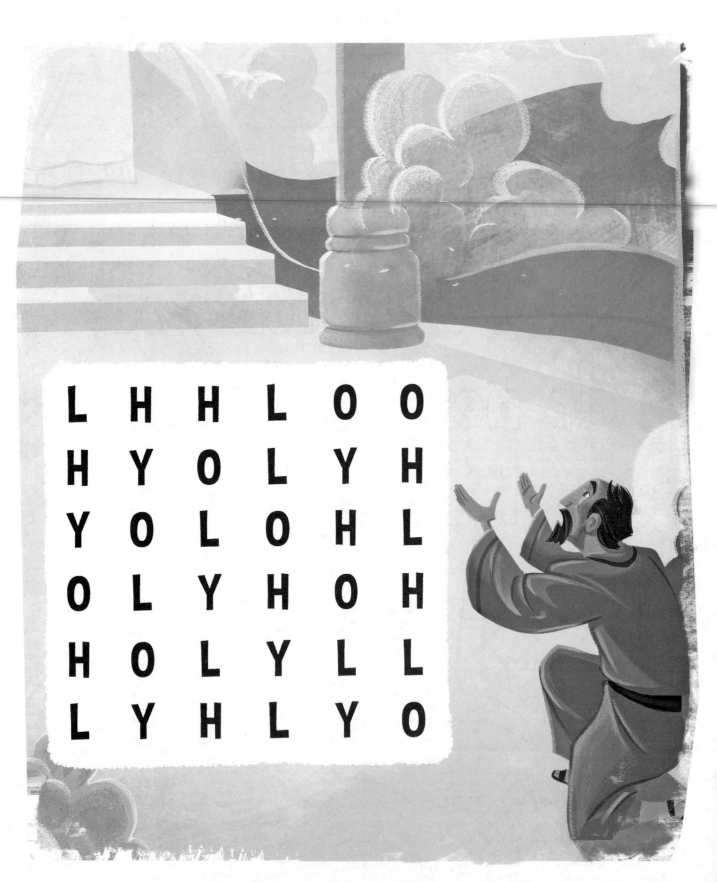

```
L  H  H  L  O  O
H  Y  O  L  Y  H
Y  O  L  O  H  L
O  L  Y  H  O  H
H  O  L  Y  L  L
L  Y  H  L  Y  O
```

Isaiah Preached About the Messiah

We all went astray like sheep; we all have turned to our own way; and the LORD has punished Him for the iniquity of us all.

–Isaiah 53:6

God Called Jeremiah

Acrostic: Called by God

Write sentences about Jeremiah using the letters of his name as the first letter for the beginning of your sentences.

J eremiah was a prophet to Judah.

E _____

R _____

E _____

M _____

I _____

A _____

H _____

Jeremiah Warned of God's Judgment

Secret Code: A Future Promise

What did God promise through the prophet Jeremiah? Use the key to decode the answer.

Example: V T M = C A T

God promised a __ __ __
G X P

and __ __ __ __ __ __
U X M M X K

__ __ __ __ __ __ __ __ .
V H O X G T G M

Find It: Tricky Hearts

Jeremiah explained that our hearts can trick us about what is right and wrong. Cross out the things that are sinful and circle the things that would please God.

Ezekiel and the Dry Bones

Maze: Dry Bones

Find the correct path to navigate through the valley of dry bones.

Hidden Message: Dry Bones

Color the 1 spaces blue, the 2 spaces yellow, and the 3 spaces brown to discover the name of a prophet who told about a future hope.

Daniel and His Friends Obeyed God

Matching: Dishes

The Babylonians took all the holy dishes, candlesticks, and other gold and silver things out of the temple to Babylon. The king had a party where the people drank from dishes meant for God's temple. Find the dishes in each group that are the same shape, and color them the same colors.

Find It: What Does Not Belong?

Examine the foods in each row. Draw an X over the food that does not belong.

Secret Code: Friends in Babylon

Decode the names of the four boys who were sent to Babylon to serve King Nebuchadnezzar.

Shadrach, Meshach, and Abednego

Color by Number

Color each section according to the number written in it. 1 = Red, 2 = Orange, 3 = Yellow, 4 = Black.

Find It: What Is Different?

Find and circle the four differences between the two pictures.

God Gave Daniel Wisdom

Hidden Message: Daniel

Color the letters in the drawing green to find a message that God gave to Daniel. Then color the rest of the picture.

Daniel Was Rescued from the Lions

Find It: The Lions' Den

Draw circles around the four sleeping lions. Draw an X on the two lions licking their lips. Draw a square around the lion scratching her ear. How many lions are in the lions' den?

Word Search: Lions' Den

Find and circle the words hidden in the puzzle.

```
A D L K H X N K S K
S A A T I O I P A Q
W N A N L N K R F F
N E O Y I D G A E Z
D I B I O E O Y T T
I A S W L U L E Z S
B E U C S E R R D U
J D A R I U S R I R
F G O D J E S U S T
A K C J P Y C N O R
```

BABYLON   LAW

DANIEL   LIONS

DARIUS   PRAYER

DEATH   RESCUE

GOD   SAFE

JESUS   SIN

KING   TRUST

When I am
AFRAID,
I will trust in
YOU.
-Psalm 56:3

Matching: Minor Prophets

Color the pictures of the minor prophets from the Old Testament. Then match the names of the people to their pictures. Can you find them on other pages in this book?

Joel

Hosea

Amos

Micah

Nahum

Jonah

Hosea, Prophet to Israel

Word Search: Hosea

Circle the key words in the puzzle.

```
M L N B F D E M L P L G
T E Z U B V G O U C E E
I E Z N O O R I H Q S M
S R H L L U F H T I A F
R Z A P H L O A M M I R
A E Y A O V Q O S V E E
E J M P G R R B F T D M
L A S I N P P U U L O O
H A E S O H F R N K F G
S S H T E S N K E K O G
```

HOSEA   JEZREEL   GOMER

PROPHET   LO-RUHAMAH   PROMISE

FAITHFUL   LO-AMMI   SIN

LOVE   ISRAEL   RETURN

Secret Code: Never Give Up

Use the key to decode the secret message about God's love.

GOD LOVES WITH A LOVE THAT NEVER GIVES UP

Maze: Go Get Gomer

Complete the maze to help Hosea get his wife, Gomer, to bring her home.

Joel, Prophet to Judah

Unscramble: Locust Focus

Unscramble the words and phrases on the locusts to form the main point of the story of Joel.

His people

God

the day

to repent

before

Lord

of the

warned

Jonah, Journey to Nineveh

Find It: Fishy Fishy

Color the biggest fish in the sea green. Color the blowfish purple. Color the striped fish orange. Color the polka-dotted fish red. Color all the other fish any color you want. How many fish are in the picture?

Maze: Jonah's Journey

Make your way through the maze to trace Jonah's journey to Nineveh.

Jonah, Prophet to Nineveh

Nahum, Prophet to Nineveh

Hidden Message: Yes or No?

Does God keep His promises? Color in the even numbers to find the answer.

1	2	7	8	1	5	1	4	3	1	7
5	6	1	4	1	8	6	2	5	6	8
7	4	3	8	7	2	4	8	7	2	4
3	9	1	6	5	1	6	2	1	5	1
8	1	4	8	3	8	2	8	4	6	1
2	5	6	2	9	6	8	4	2	8	5
4	7	8	4	5	1	5	6	7	9	1

What promise did Nehemiah trust God to keep?

_____

_____

_____

_____

Prophets Told About Jesus' Birth

Isaiah 7:1–14; 9:1–7; 11:1–5; Micah 5:2

Hidden Message: Book Name

Color each space with a dot in it to find the name of a very special book. Use the same color for all spaces with dots. Color the other spaces in different colors. *Hint: This book tells us about God and Jesus.*

For a child
will be born for us,
a son will be given to us,
and the government
will be on his shoulders.
He will be named
WONDERFUL COUNSELOR,
MIGHTY GOD,
ETERNAL FATHER,
PRINCE OF PEACE.

–Isaiah 9:6

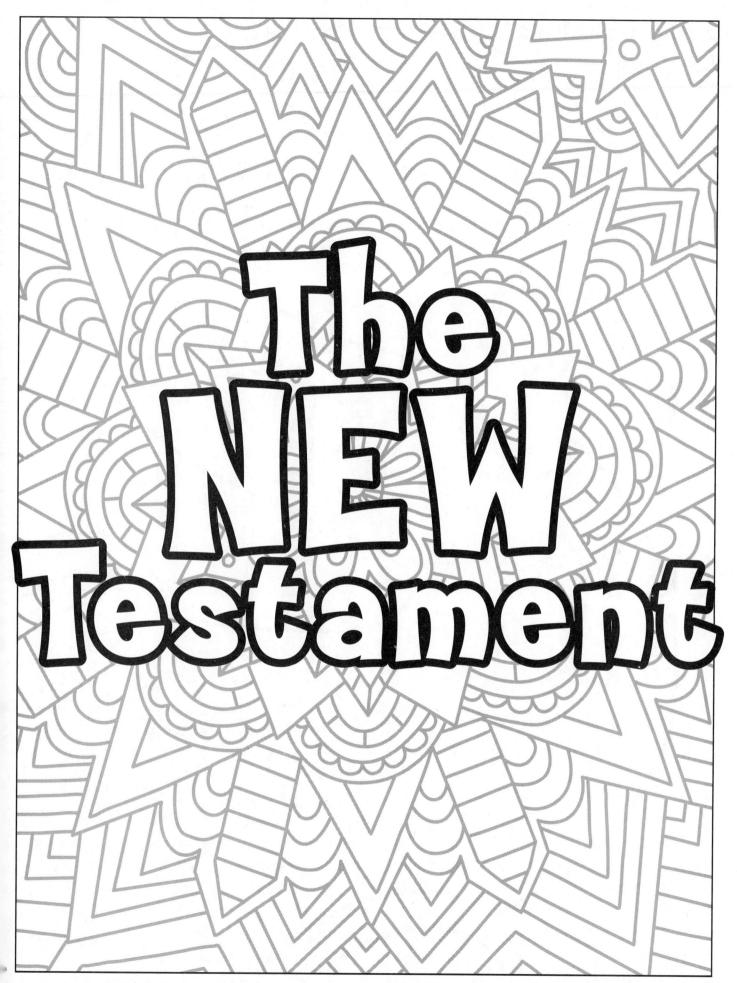

The NEW Testament

From Abraham to Jesus

Matthew 1:1–17; Luke 3:23–38

Maze: The Family of Jesus

Make your way through the maze to connect the family in order from Adam all the way to Jesus.

An Angel Spoke to Zechariah

Mary Was Visited by an Angel

Secret Code: A Special Purpose

Use the key to fill in the blanks and crack the code.

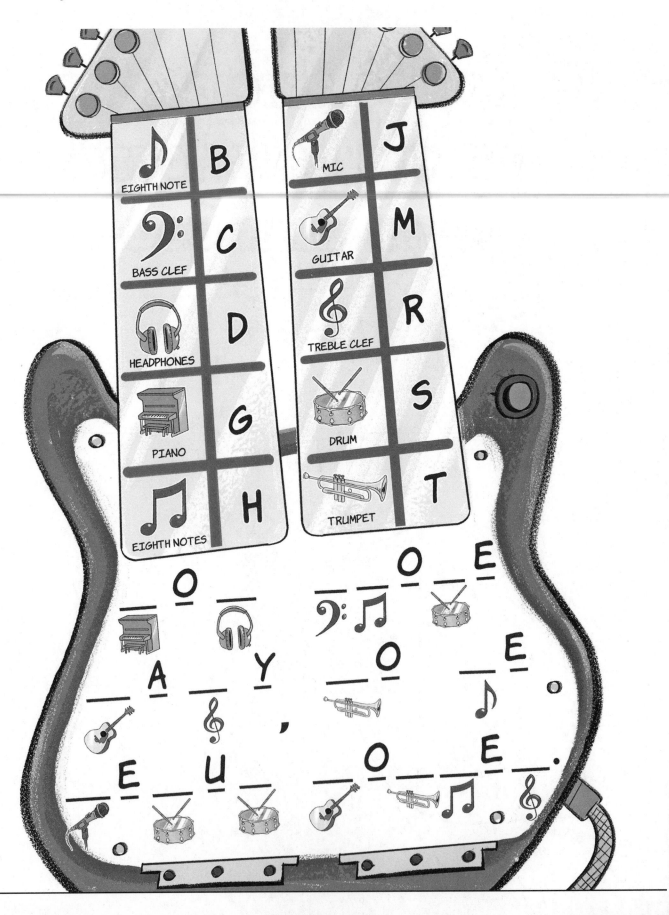

Hidden Message: Joseph's Dream

Starting with the letter J, color in every other letter to see what the angel told Joseph to name Mary's baby.

Find It: What Is Different?

Circle eight things that are different in the bottom picture.

Mary Visited Elizabeth

Mary Visited Elizabeth

Complete the maze to get Mary to Elizabeth's house.

Finish

Start

John the Baptist Was Born

Mary and Joseph Traveled to Bethlehem

Maze: The Way to Bethlehem

Find the path that will take Mary and Joseph to Bethlehem.

start

finish

Jesus Was Born

Angels Told the Shepherds of Jesus' Birth

Connect the Stars: The Angels Praised God

Draw a line to connect the stars with words to find out what the angels said when Jesus was born. Start at the top and move to the bottom.

Secret Code: Mary's Motto

Use the shape code to put the vowels in the right places to see what Mary said in Luke 1:38.

Word Search: Jesus Was Born

Find and circle the key words form the word list in the puzzle.

Word List

ANGELS
BABY
BETHLEHEM
CENSUS
DAVID
EARTH
GLORY
GOOD NEWS
HEAVEN
JESUS
JOSEPH
KING
LORD
MARY
MESSIAH
PEACE
SAVIOR
SHEEP
SHEPHERDS

```
S C E N S U S D S J S A
V D K S M Z S R W R H N
J Z R A U A V O E D E G
H O R E V S Y L N I E E
E Y S I H R E H D V P L
H A O E O P A J O A P S
R R R L P I E U O D S W
S J G T S H A H G W Z A
E O X S H K Y Z S N U P
S O E N E V A E H L I L
C M P E A C E Y B A B K
M E H E L H T E B D A M
```

Find It: Jesus in the Stable

Circle the donkeys. Draw a square around the cows. Draw an X on the sheep.

Connect the Dots

Connect the dots to see one of the animals that was at the stable where Jesus was born.

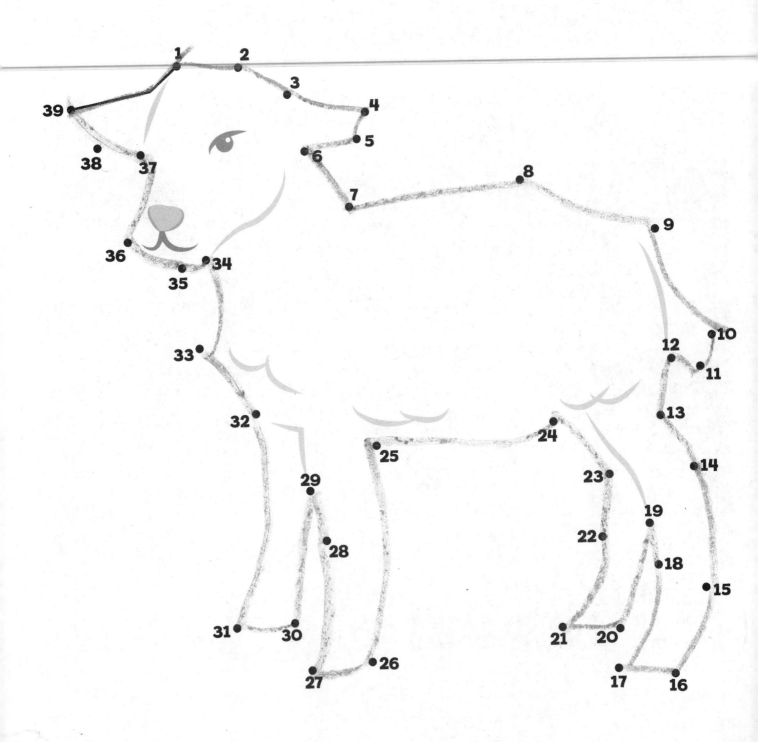

Fill in the Blanks: Good News!

Use words from the word list to fill in the blanks. You may use some words more than once.

Word List

BABY

EARTH

GOOD NEWS

HEAVEN

JESUS

SAVIOR

The birth of _____ was _____ _____!

_____ was not an ordinary _____.

He is God's Son, sent to _____ from _____.

_____ came into the world to save people

from sin and to be their _____ forever.

Jesus Was Dedicated

The Wise Men Visited Jesus

Maze: Follow the Star

Color the bigger stars shown in the key to lead the wise men to Jesus.

Maze: Help the Wise Men Find Jesus

Find the one path that will lead the wise men to Jesus.

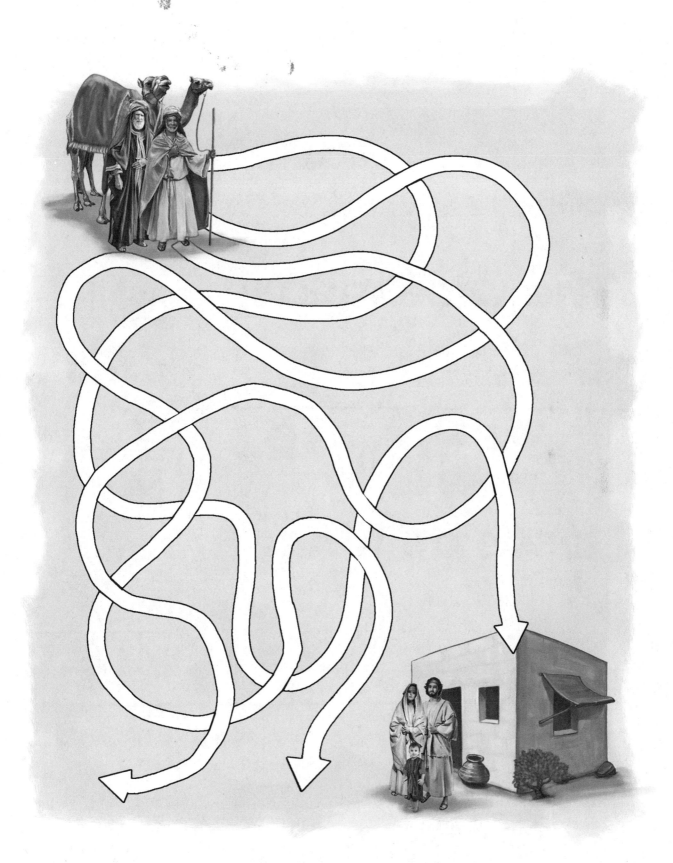

The wise men _____ Jesus as King.

Jesus at the Temple

And Jesus increased in wisdom and stature, and in favor with God and with people.
-Luke 2:52

Secret Code: Where Was Jesus?

For each blank, use the direction shown in the arrows to go forward or backward one letter in the alphabet to fill in the blanks and find the secret message.

A B C D E F G H I J K L M N O P Q R S T U V W X Y Z

Didn't you know I had to be

I N _ M Y
(H→ O←   N← Z←)

F A T H E R ' S
(G← B← S→ G← F← S← R→)

H O U S E ?
(G→ P← V← R→ F←)

Luke 2:49

C→ = D   S← = R

221

Just as you want others to do for you, do the same for them.
-Luke 6:31

Find It: Jesus in the Temple

Look at the smaller picture of Jesus. Then find Him in the crowds of the larger picture.

John the Baptist

Fill in the Blanks: Who Am I?

Use your Bible to answer the following questions. Unscramble the circled letters to find out whom the prophet Malachi spoke about.

Who Am I?

1. In which testament is the Book of Malachi?

◯__ _____

2. What is the name of the sixth book of the Bible?

___◯___

3. How many books are in the Old Testament?

_____◯____

4. Which book comes after the Book of Isaiah?

◯_____

Malachi said God was going to send a messenger to get people ready for the promised Messiah.

The messenger's name was

___ ___ ___ ___ ___ .

Maze: Help Jesus Get to John the Baptist

Find the correct path from Jesus to John the Baptist.

Jesus Was Baptized

Connect the Dots: Baptism

Connect the dots to finish the picture. Then complete the sentence:

_____ obeyed God by being baptized by John.

Finish the Picture: Dove

Ask an adult to help you trace your hands to give the dove wings and tail feathers. Then color the picture.

Unscramble: Messenger Mix-Up

The names of these messengers are all mixed up! Can you sort them out? Unscramble the letters of the messengers' names and write them in the blanks.

CHIMALA

_____ was a messenger—a prophet—who told God's people to repent. He also told about another messenger God would send.

HOJN

_____ the Baptist called people to repent and to get ready for a final Messenger.

_____, the final Messenger, brought good news of salvation.

JUSES

What Order?: Great, Greater, Greatest!

For each row, number the items from 1 to 3. (3 = great, 2 = greater, 1 = greatest). Then compare your answers with a partner. Do you agree on what is great, greater, and the greatest?

bowling	baseball	football
pizza	cookies	carrots
fall	summer	winter
John	Jesus	lion

Crossword: Jesus Was Baptized

Use the clues and key words to fill in the crossword puzzle.

ACROSS

2. the messenger who got people ready for Jesus (John 1:23)
3. to turn away from sin and turn to God (Mark 1:4)
6. the place where Jesus was baptized (Matthew 3:13)
8. The Spirit came down like this animal (Matthew 3:16)
9. a way to show that a person's sins are washed away (Mark 1:4)
10. Jesus never did this (Matthew 3:14-15)

DOWN

1. what Jesus baptizes with (Mark 1:8)
4. John called Jesus this name (John 1:29)
5. John said he was not the promised _____. (John 1:20)
7. what John baptized with (Mark 1:8)

KEY WORDS:	
dove	baptize
Holy Spirit	Messiah
sinned	repent
John	Jordan River
Lamb of God	water

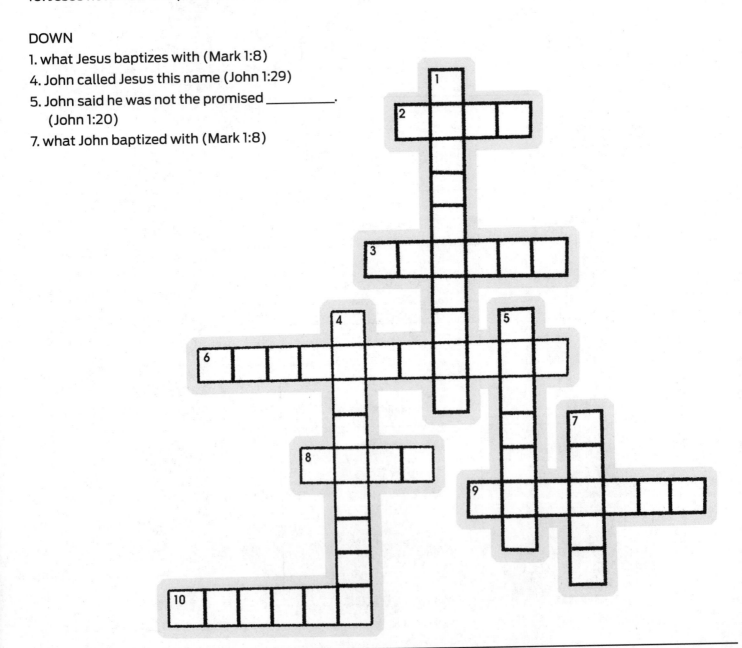

Matching: Who Did It?

Draw a line connecting the picture to the person the picture is about, John or Jesus.

JESUS IS THE MESSIAH.

PROPHETS SAID JESUS WOULD
BE BORN IN BETHLEHEM.

JOHN WAS BORN
WHEN HIS PARENTS
WERE VERY OLD.

JOHN THE BAPTIST

JESUS

GOD SAID JESUS IS
HIS BELOVED SON.

JOHN GOT PEOPLE
READY FOR JESUS.

JOHN SAID HE WAS
NOT THE MESSIAH.

Jesus Was Tempted

Matthew 4:1–11; Mark 1:12–13; Luke 4:1–13

Then Jesus told him, "Go away, Satan! For it is written: Worship the Lord your God, and serve only him." —Matthew 4:10

Find It: Hidden Food

Use the key to find the foods hidden in the picture. Circle them.

What Order?: Jesus Was Tempted

Number the pictures in the order the events happened. Then label each picture with one of these Scripture references describing the scene:

Matthew 4:2   Matthew 4:4   Matthew 4:5-6   Matthew 4:8-9

Secret Code: Jesus Said . . .

Use the code to fill in the words Jesus said when He was tempted to sin.

Man must not live on

_____ _____ _____ _____ _____ alone

but on every _____ _____ _____ _____

that comes from the mouth of

_____ _____ _____ .

Matthew 4:4

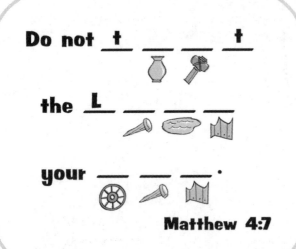

Do not t ___ ___ t

the L ___ ___ ___

your ___ ___ ___ .

Matthew 4:7

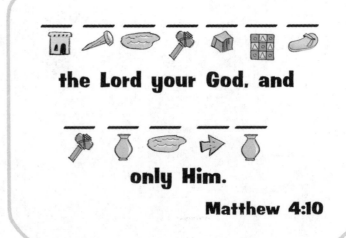

_____ _____ _____ _____ _____ _____ _____

the Lord your God, and

_____ _____ _____ _____ _____

only Him.

Matthew 4:10

Jesus Called His Disciples

The Twelve Disciples

Color the circles with names of the twelve disciples yellow. Color the rest of the circles with as many colors as you can.

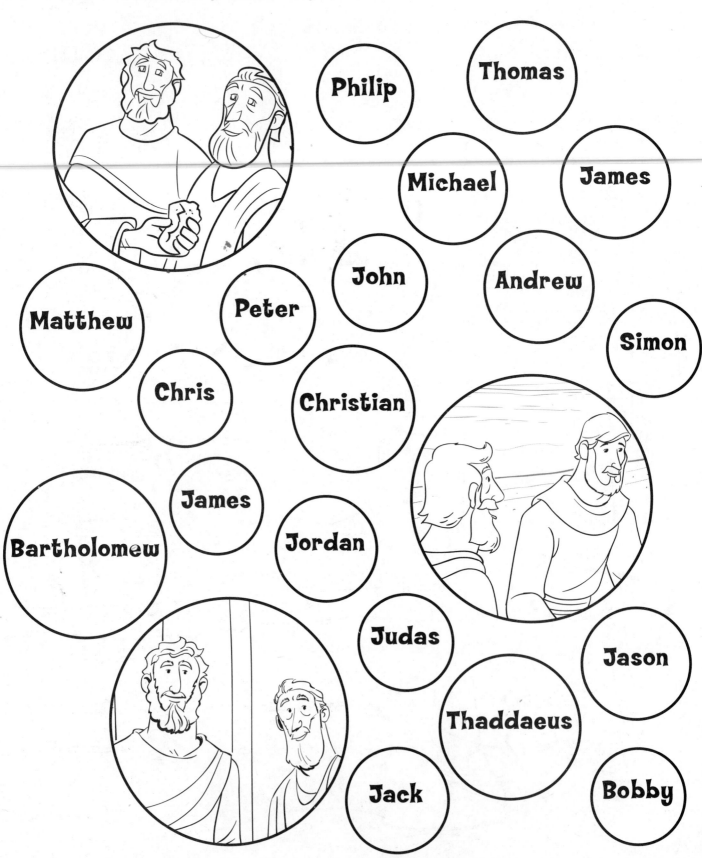

Philip

Thomas

Michael

James

John

Andrew

Matthew

Peter

Simon

Chris

Christian

James

Bartholomew

Jordan

Judas

Jason

Thaddaeus

Jack

Bobby

Maze: Jesus Called the Twelve Disciples

Help the disciples find their way through the maze to Jesus.

By this everyone will know that you are my disciples, if you love one another.
–John 13:35

Jesus Turned Water to Wine

Secret Code: Signs and Wonders

To fill in the missing words, first find the water jug (A, B, or C) and then count down to the corresponding word (1, 2, 3 ...). *For example, C1 = He.*

_____   _____   _____
   B2   C3   A1

_____   _____   _____
   A4   A2   B1

_____   _____
   A3   C5

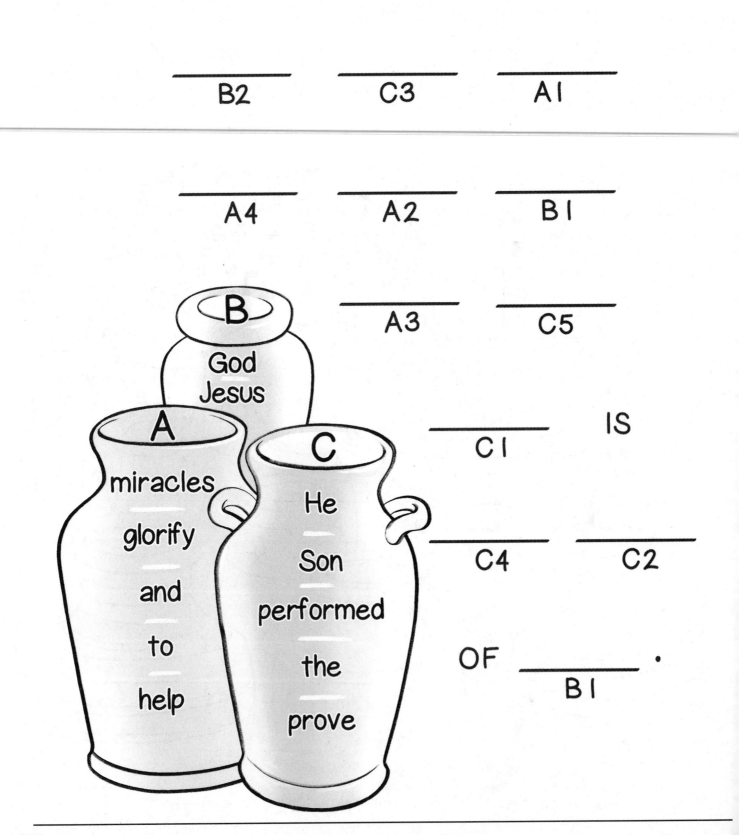

_____   IS
  C1

_____   _____
  C4   C2

OF _____ .
      B1

Maze: Signs and Wonders

Follow the maze to figure out which letters complete the bottom word.

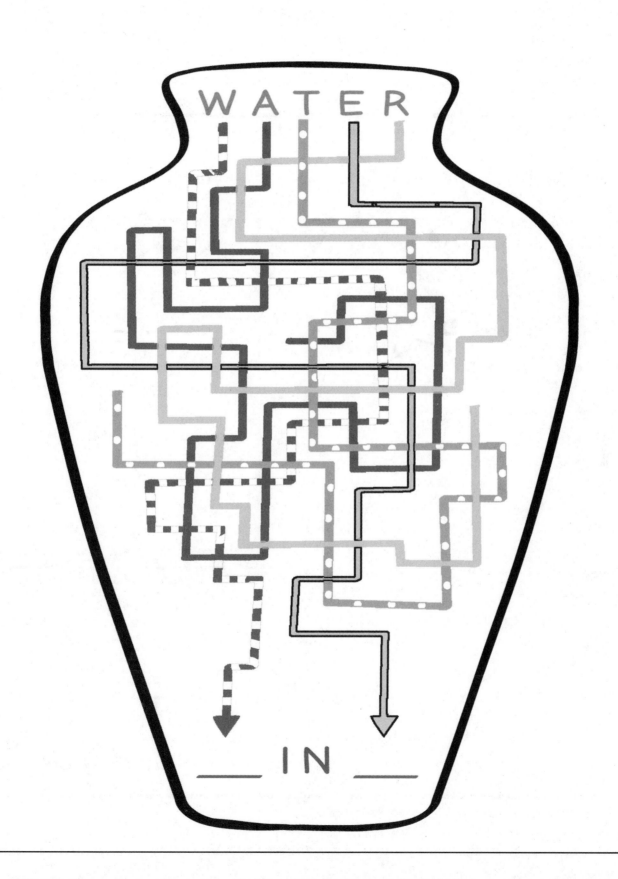

Connect the Dots: Water to Wine

Draw lines to connect the dots in numerical order to reveal a picture. Color the picture.

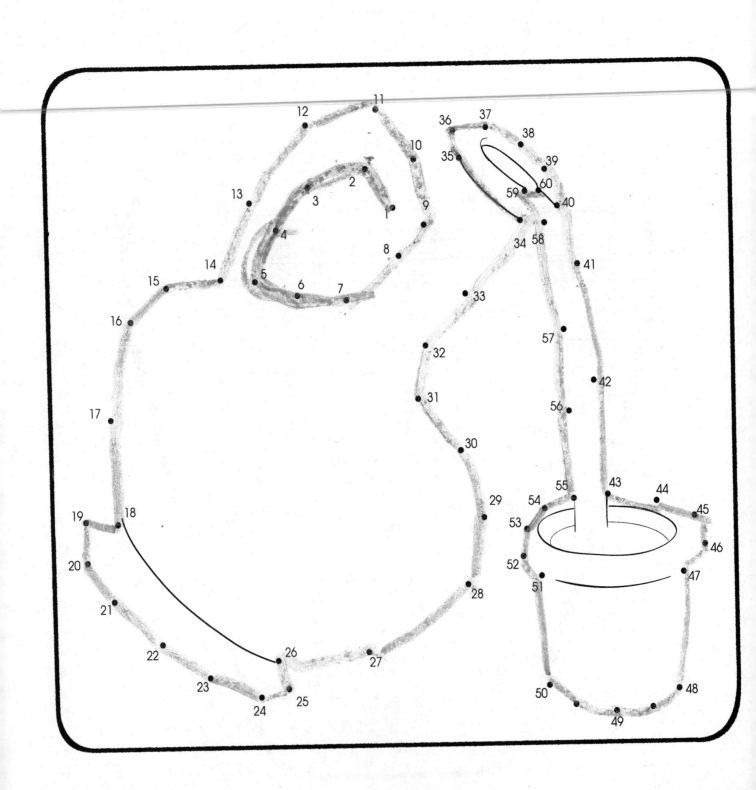

Jesus Met Nicodemus

Find It: What Is Different?

Look at the pictures. Circle the eleven differences in the second picture.

Maze: The Way to Jesus

Complete the maze to help Nicodemus get to Jesus.

Jesus

Finish

Start

Nicodemus

Fill in the Blanks: One Way to Jesus

Use the words in the arrow to fill in the missing words of the verse. *Tip: Not all of the words will be used.* Color in the rest of the arrows.

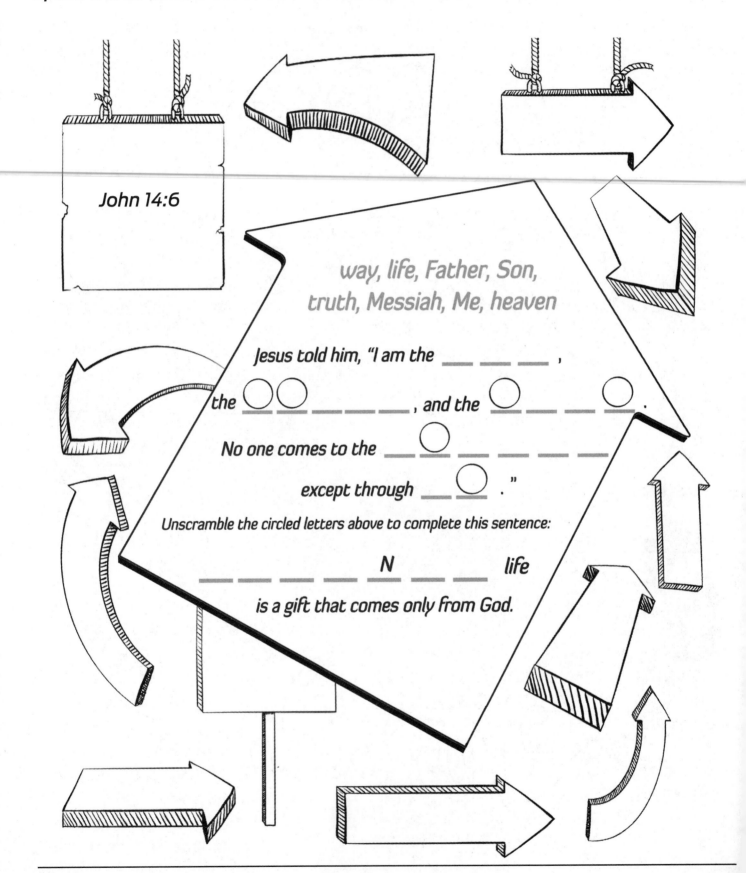

John 14:6

way, life, Father, Son, truth, Messiah, Me, heaven

Jesus told him, "I am the ___ ___ ___ ,

the ⃝⃝_____ , and the ⃝_____ ⃝.

No one comes to the ⃝___ _____

except through ___⃝ ."

Unscramble the circled letters above to complete this sentence:

_____ _____ N _____ _____ life

is a gift that comes only from God.

Find It: What Does Not Belong?

Find and circle the items in the picture below that don't belong.

Jesus Met a Samaritan Woman

Unscramble: Well Words

List the words you can spell from the letters in the well. Use the letters to fill in the blanks on the well.

_____

_____

_____

Jesus told the Samaritan
woman He is the

_ _ _ _ _ _ _ _

What Order?: Finish the Pattern

Look at the pictures in each row. Circle the picture that comes next in the pattern.

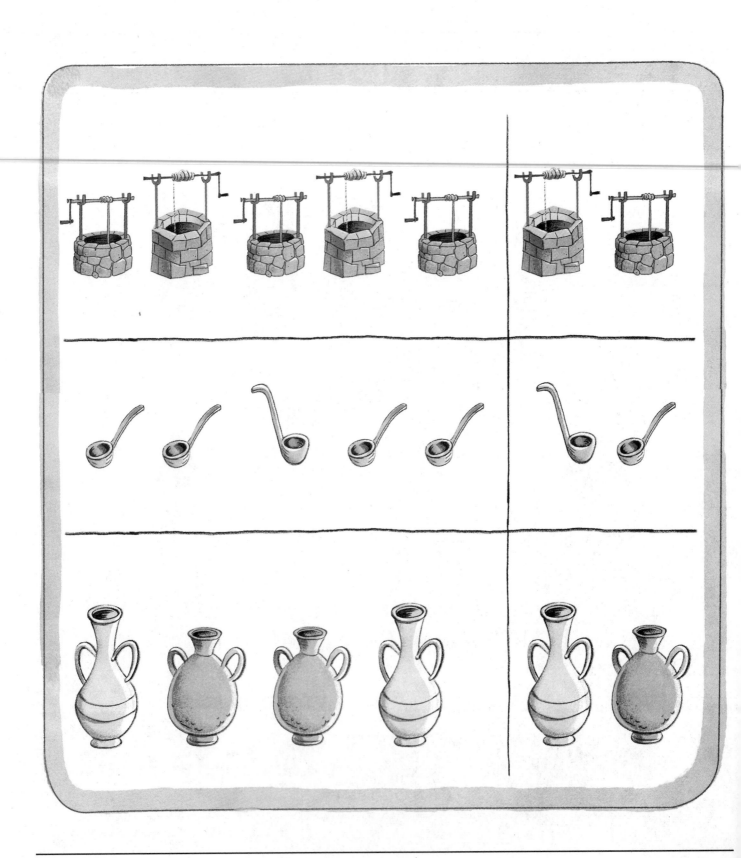

Hidden Message: Never Thirst Again

Jesus offered the Samaritan woman something no one else could give her. Color the 1 spaces blue and the 2 spaces yellow.

What did Jesus say He could give the woman?

_____ _____

Secret Code: A Promise from Jesus

Fill in the blanks in the scripture verse using the letter code below. Ex. E=V.

You will know the

_ _ _ _ _ ,
G I F G S

and the truth will set you free.
-John 8:32

Letter Code

A	B	C	D	E	F	G	H	I	J	K	L	M	N	O	P	Q	R	S	T	U	V	W	X	Y	Z
Z	Y	X	W	V	U	T	S	R	Q	P	O	N	M	L	K	J	I	H	G	F	E	D	C	B	A

Matching: Bibles

Draw lines to connect matching Bibles.

Jesus Drove out Unclean Spirits

Word Search: Power Up

Jesus has power over evil. How many times can you find the word *power* in the puzzle below?

```
W E R O W P R O O P
P O W E R R R O E W O
O R E P E E P W R W
W P O W E R P O E E
E R O E P P O W E R
R P R W O R W P R O
W O W R W O E O P E
R W O O E W R O W O
O E P R R O W E O P
P R E P O P O W E R
```

Acrostic: Power Play

In the blanks below, write a word or sentence that starts with each of the different letters in the word *power*.

The Sermon on the Mount

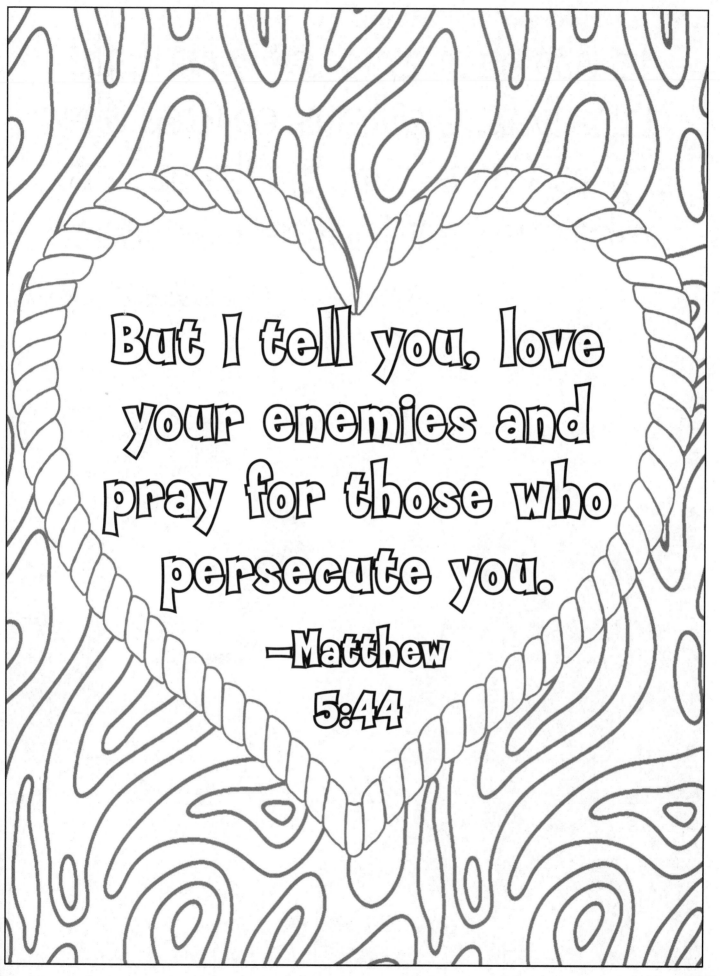

But I tell you, love your enemies and pray for those who persecute you. —Matthew 5:44

In the same way, let your light shine before others, so that they may see your good works and give glory to your Father in heaven.

–Matthew 5:16

Fill in the Blanks: To Seek and Save

Fill in the missing vowels—A, E, I, O, and U—to finish the sentences.

J__s__s c__m__ t__ s___k
__nd s__v__ th__ l__st.
H__ c__m__ __ft__r
__s–s__nn__rs wh__ d__
n__t d__s__rv__ H__m—
__nd H__ r__sc___s __s
fr__m s__n. J__s__s d___d
__n th__ cr__ss f__r ___r
s__n, __nd H__ __s gl__d
wh__n w__ r__p__nt __nd
tr__st __n H__m.

Hidden Message: Missing Word

Color the spaces with dots blue to find the word to finish the sentence. Write the word in the blanks when you find it. Color in the rest of the spaces using as many colors as you can.

For the Son of Man has come to seek and to save the

_____ _____ _____ _____.

- Luke 19:10

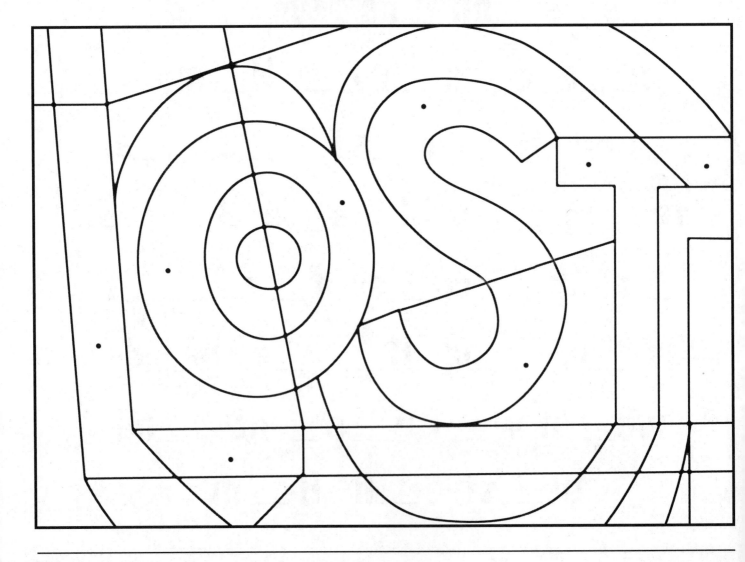

Fill in the Blanks: The Lord's Prayer

Fill in the missing words to the prayer below.

Our Father in _____,
Your name be honored as holy.
Your _____ come. Your will be
done on earth as it is in heaven.
Give us today our daily _____.
And forgive us our debts, as we
also have forgiven our debtors.
And do not bring us into _____,
but deliver us from the evil one.
For Yours is the kingdom
and the _____ and the
_____ forever. Amen.

Jesus Healed Peter's Mother-in-Law

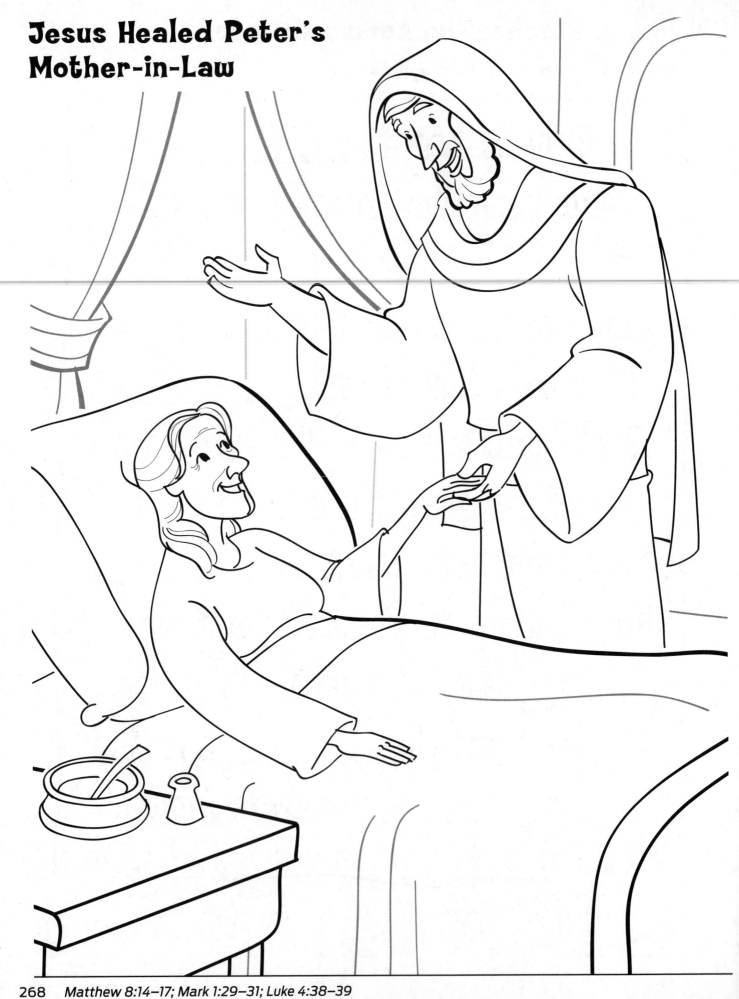

Matthew 8:14–17; Mark 1:29–31; Luke 4:38–39

Jesus Cleansed a Leper

Jesus Healed an Official's Son

Jesus Calmed the Storm

Jesus Drove Out Demons

Matthew 8:28–34; Mark 5:1–20; Luke 8:26–39

Fill in the Blanks: Finish the Story

Fill in the blanks using the words at the bottom of the page.

Jesus met a man living in the region of the _____.

The man had an _____ _____ inside him. Jesus _____

the evil spirit to come out. The spirits inside the man

_____ Jesus not to send them away. Jesus allowed

the evil spirits to leave the man and go into the _____.

The pigs ran down the _____ and into the _____.

The people were _____ , and they asked Jesus to

_____. Jesus told the man to tell his _____ and

family members how the Lord had _____ him. Jesus

has _____ over evil. One day, Jesus will end evil _____.

afraid	begged	evil spirit	commanded
friends	forever	helped	Gerasenes
hill	leave	pigs	power sea

Four Friends Helped

Matthew 9:1–8; Mark 2:1–12; Luke 5:17–26

Secret Code: Jesus the Healer

Use the grid to fill in the blanks and answer the big picture question: What did Jesus heal people from?

Jesus healed people from

$\underline{\text{S}}$ $\underline{\text{I}}$ $\underline{\text{C}}$ $\underline{\text{K}}$ $\underline{\text{N}}$ $\underline{\text{E}}$ $\underline{\text{S}}$ $\underline{\text{S}}$,
A1   C1   B1   B2   D2   D3   A1   A1

$\underline{\text{S}}$ $\underline{\text{I}}$ $\underline{\text{N}}$, and
A1   C1   D2

$\underline{\text{D}}$ $\underline{\text{E}}$ $\underline{\text{A}}$ $\underline{\text{T}}$ $\underline{\text{H}}$.
C3   D3   A3   B3   C2

	A	B	C	D
1	S	C	I	U
2	O	K	H	N
3	A	T	D	E

Jesus Healed a Man's Hand

Matthew 12:9–14; Mark 3:1–6; Luke 6:6–11

The Parable of the Sower

Maze: Good Soil

Trace the four paths using different colors. Which path leads to the good soil?

Rocky soil

Soil by the path

Soil among the weeds

Good soil

Unscramble: Scattered Seeds

Unscramble the seeds to discover the message.

A _____ is a _____ that
PBALERA   SOYRT

Jesus told to _____ people
PLEH

understand the _____ of
NIGKMOD

_____.
OGD

Jesus told a _____ about
BLEPARA

How people _____ to the
PONDSER

_____.
PELSOG

What Order?: The Growing Seed

Put the numbers 1–5 in the boxes to show the order in which a plant grows.

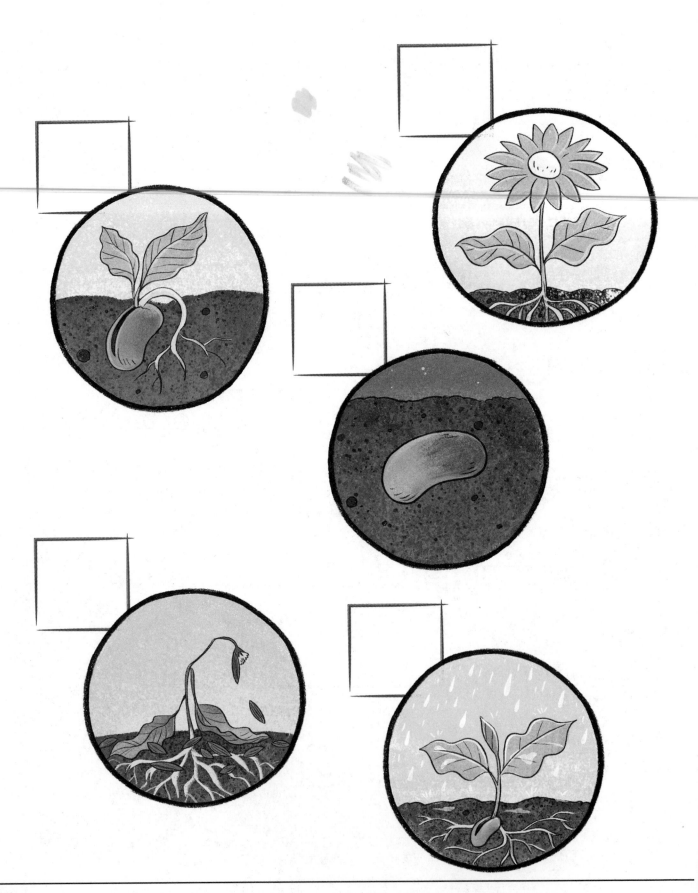

Jesus Provided Bread from Heaven

Crossword: Challenge 5000

Use the clues to complete the crossword puzzle.
Words: compassion, five thousand, evening, two, twelve, disciples, sick

4. how many men Jesus fed (Matthew 14:21)

5. who asked Jesus to send the people away (Matthew 14:15)

7. the time of day when the crowds were fed (Matthew 14:15)

1. number of baskets full of leftovers (Matthew 14:20)

2. what Jesus felt when He saw a huge crowd (Matthew 14:14)

3. how many fish the disciples had (Matthew 14:14)

6. Jesus healed these people (Matthew 14:14)

Maze: Feeding the Five Thousand

Help the little boy with 2 fish and 5 loaves of bread get to Jesus so everyone can eat!

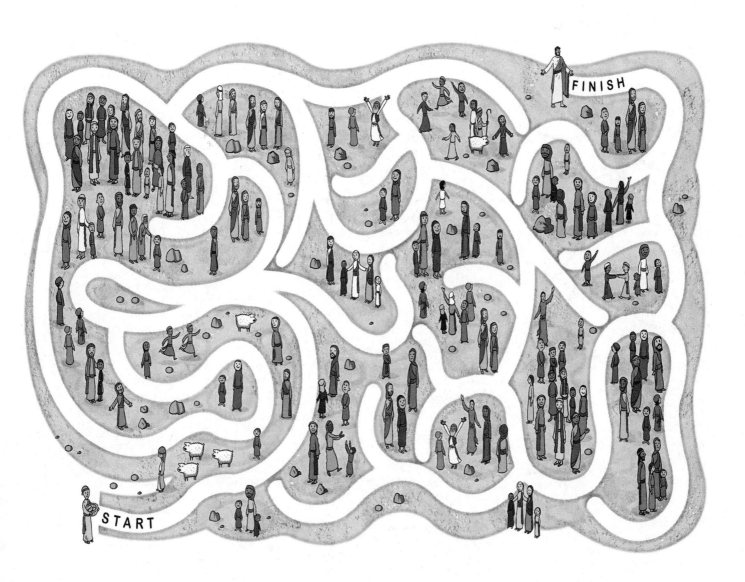

Jesus Fed Five Thousand

Matthew 14:13–21; Mark 6:30–44; Luke 9:10–17; John 6:1–14

A Child Helps Jesus

Color the boy who brought his lunch to help Jesus feed the people.

Lots of Loaves

Count the number of loaves of bread. Color them in to make sure you have counted them all.

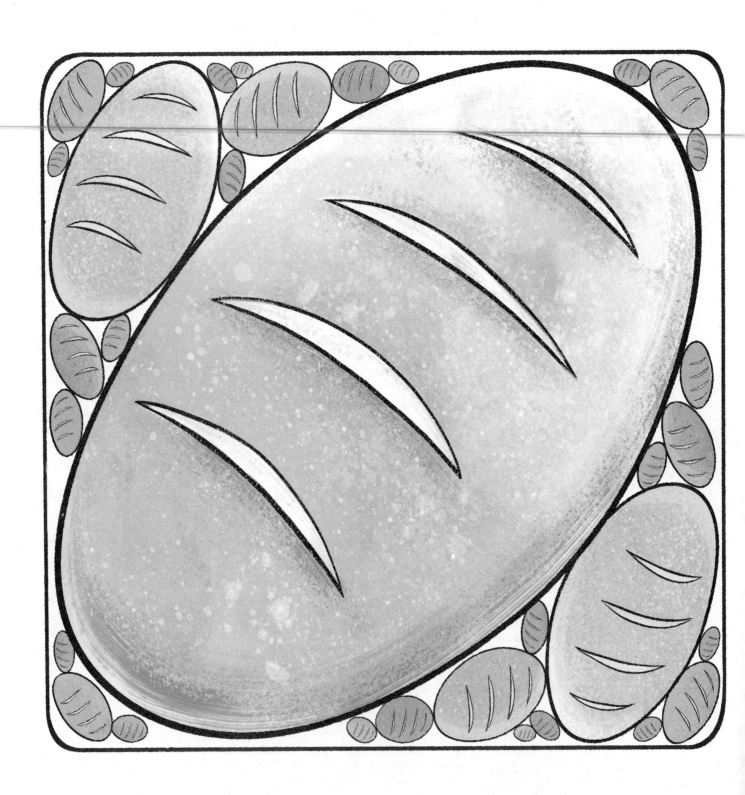

Jesus Walked on Water

Hidden Message: Calling Out

Color the letters that have a dot to read what Peter said.

Maze: The A-MAZE-ing Walk

Complete the maze to guide Peter from the boat to Jesus.

The Good Samaritan

Luke 10:25–37

Word Search: The Good Samaritan

Find and circle the key words found in the Bible story about the parable of the good Samaritan.

```
L L A W Y E R D C R Q G
O F C Q J R Z Y M B I Z
V P T S N E I G H B O R
E G Q H A P T E Q F G D
H S C A N M E O Q L D A
Q E T E R N A L L I F E
J D L B I E C R S N A X
J O F P J I H K I U T M
E N U L I D E Q K T L R
S K N I L N R B B P A L
U E W U J G G H E O G N
S Y O V O R O B B E R S
```

LAWYER

TEACHER

ETERNAL LIFE

LOVE

NEIGHBOR

SAMARITAN

ROBBERS

DONKEY

JESUS

HELPING

The Parable of the Lost Son

Luke 15:11–32

Find It: Lost and Found

Search the picture to find the lost son, the sheep, and the ten coins.

The Pharisee and the Tax Collector

Hidden Message: The Pharisee and the Tax Collector

Color the squares containing the number 8 to reveal two key words about the story of the Pharisee and the tax collector.

Jesus Loves the Children

Matthew 19:13–15; Mark 10:13–16; Luke 18:15–17

Maze: Jesus Loves the Children

Follow the path to help Jesus bring bread to the little girl.

Jesus Healed a Blind Man

Matthew 20:29–34; Mark 10:46–52; Luke 18:35–43

Jesus and Zacchaeus

Count the Coins

Zacchaeus tricked people to take their money. Add up the value of the coins he took in the picture.

Find It: Where's Zacchaeus?

Use the key to find Zacchaeus in the picture. Circle Zacchaeus.

KEY

Matching: People of the Parables

A parable is a story that has a lesson. Match the pictures with the descriptions of these parables told by Jesus. Can you find these people on other pages in this book?

faithful servant

sower

wedding feast

rich young ruler

wicked tenant

unmerciful servant

The Unmerciful Servant

Secret Code: Coin Counting

Circle the bag in each row with the correct number of coins. Then write the corresponding letter in the blank at the bottom to reveal a key word from the Bible story.

is not getting the punishment you deserve,
but being shown kindness instead.

Connect the Dots: Partner Game

Find a friend. Take turns connecting two dots with a line. If you complete a box, mark it as yours and go again.

The Rich Young Ruler

Mark 10:17–34; Luke 18:18–34

Finish the Picture: Following Jesus

In the circles below, draw some things that you would give up if it would please Jesus.

The Wicked Tenants

Word Search: Vine Words

Find and circle the words from the word bank.

C J R R P G V O E Q Y L A I Y
X Q W C A B F Z B G E Z A A X
U S P J V Z M E N H R F Y O T
D W O N B Y G P V V S C V E P
D O R T N E W A B E I V W H C L
S L O Y W I C K E D I W X U J
O P L P S E L Y Z G N P R K O
A J F U H O T L G E E U H L G
Z B S D O W N C Q R Y T B Z A
T E N A N T A Z J J A H Z V I
J S L N E S T Y R E R P W R R
O Z C Y F O T C D J D O E H J
Q Z W G X Q A R G V E V A S B
H A C Z K P C P Z S T W S K W
G X F V O A K O L D W H T Y Y

WORD SEARCH:

Tenant
Jesus
Vineyard
Grapes
Son
Wicked
Attack
Death

Unscramble: Accept or Reject

Unscramble the names of books of the Bible. Then fill in the numbered boxes to decode the message.

NEGSEIS
  1 2   3 4

TACS
    5   6

LANDIE
  7   8

WATTHEM
        9   10

MANSRO
  11 12

SEGDUJ
  13 14

1 12 7   10 4 8 8   13 14 7 1 2

6 9 12 3 2   10 9 12

11 2 13 2 5 6   13 2 3 14 3.

_____ _____ _____ _____

_____ _____ _____ _____

Jesus Had Power over Death

Unscramble: Jesus Is . . .

Unscramble the following words and fill in the blanks to reveal what Jesus said about Himself.

CETUORSIRRN   **FILE**

Jesus said, "I am the

_ _ _ _ _ _ _ _ _ _ _ _

and the

_ _ _ _ ."

(John 11:25)

Jesus Resurrected Lazarus

Use the color key to complete the picture. Fill each section with the color assigned to the number in it.

Color Key:
1- Blue
2- Brown
3- Tan
4- Gray
5- Green
6- Black

Parable of the Wedding Feast

Matthew 22:1–14

Finish the Picture: What's on Your Plate?

Draw what you would like to eat at a feast.

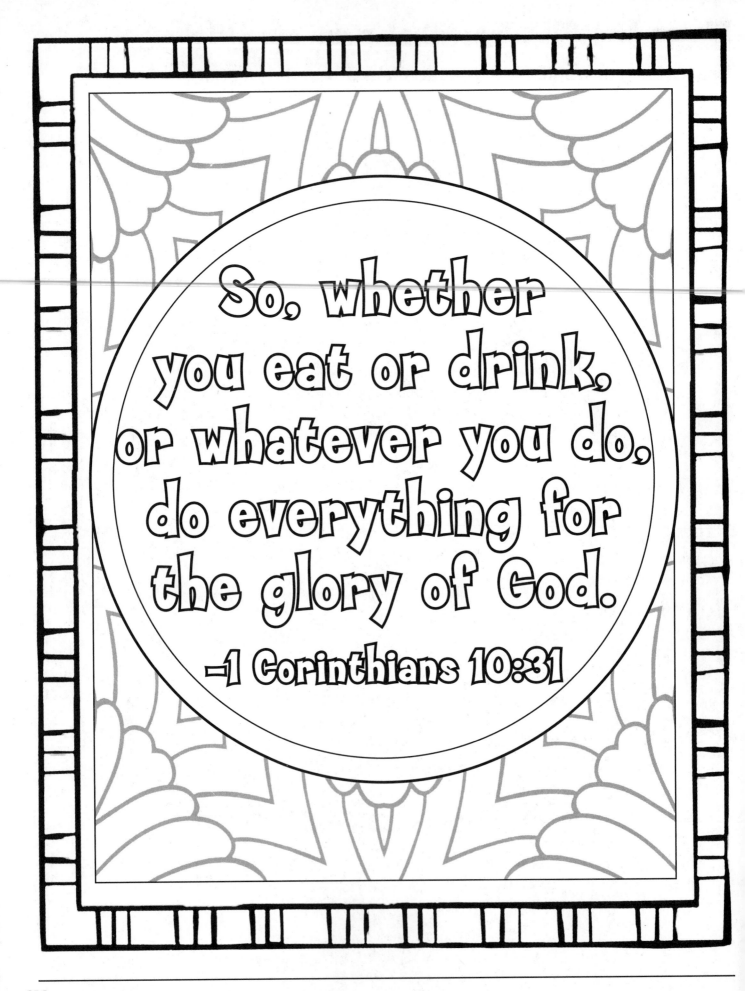

So, whether you eat or drink, or whatever you do, do everything for the glory of God.

-1 Corinthians 10:31

Maze: Wedding Feast

Help the boy make his way through the maze to the wedding feast.

Parable of the Faithful Servant

Matthew 24:45–51; Luke 12:42–48

Hidden Message: Loyal and True

Color all the letters using the key below. Find the word that means "loyal and true."

1. blue
2. red
3. green
4. yellow

Parable of the Talents

Matthew 25:14–30; Luke 19:11–27

Secret Code: The Happy Master

Use the two numbers under the blank to find the word in the chart that goes in the blank. Go across the bottom of the chart to the first number for the blank, then go up to the second number to find the right word. Ex. (6, 4) = Jesus

Points _____ _____ _____ _____ _____ _____
        (1,9)   (3,3)   (4,5)   (7,1)   (8,6)   (9,8)

Matching: The Lessons of Jesus

Number each picture to match the lesson below that Jesus taught. Color the pictures.

1. Matthew 5:16— "In the same way, let your light shine before others, so that they may see your good works and give glory to your Father in heaven."

2. Matthew 7:24— "Therefore, everyone who hears these words of mine and acts on them will be like a wise man who built his house on the rock."

3. Matthew 6:28— "And why do you worry about clothes? Observe how the wildflowers of the field grow: They don't labor or spin thread."

4. John 6:35–"I am the bread of life," Jesus told them. "No one who comes to me will ever be hungry, and no one who believes in me will ever be thirsty again."

5. Luke 15:8— "Or what woman who has ten silver coins, if she loses one coin, does not light a lamp, sweep the house, and search carefully until she finds it?"

The Triumphal Entry

Maze: Journey to Jerusalem

Complete the maze to remember that Jesus rode a donkey to get to Jerusalem.

Start

Finish

Fill in the Blanks: Palm Branch Code

Starting with A, number all of the palm branches. Then write the letter that goes with each number in the boxes below to find what the people said when Jesus came to Jerusalem.

Connect the Dots: Triumphal Entry

Connect the dots to reveal something Jesus saw on His ride into Jerusalem.

Maze: Palm Branch Crossing

Find the path for Jesus to follow into Jerusalem. You may only travel across palm branches that match. Start on the top row and move down to the bottom row. Some moves may be diagonal.

Start

Finish

Jesus Cleansed the Temple

Matthew 21:12–17; Mark 11:15–19; Luke 19:45–48; John 2:13–16

The Widow's Gift

Jesus Was Anointed

Matthew 26:6–13; Mark 14:3–9; John 12:1–8

Preparation for Passover

The Last Supper

Matthew 26:20–30; Mark 14:17–26; Luke 22:14–23; John 13:21–30

Hidden Message: Jesus' Commandment

Color all the spaces with dots red to find the hidden word. Color in the rest of the spaces using as many colors as you can.

"This is my command:

one another as I have loved you." –John 15:12

Find It: What Does Not Belong?

Circle the objects that do not belong in the picture.

No one has greater love than this: to lay down his life for his friends.

-John 15:13

Hidden Message: Talk to Jesus

Color in the spaces according to the key to find a way that you can talk to Jesus any time.

☐ *BLUE*   △*YELLOW*   ▭*RED*   ○*GREEN*

Fill in the Blanks: A Prayer Promise

Fill in the blanks with the words below to find a promise from Jesus.

"And if you _____, you will _____

whatever you _____ for in _____."

Jesus Was Arrested

Matthew 26:47–56; Mark 14:43–50; Luke 22:47–53; John 18:1–14

Jesus' Crucifixion

Maze: Crown of Thorns

Find the path through the thorns that goes from start to finish.

Start

Finish

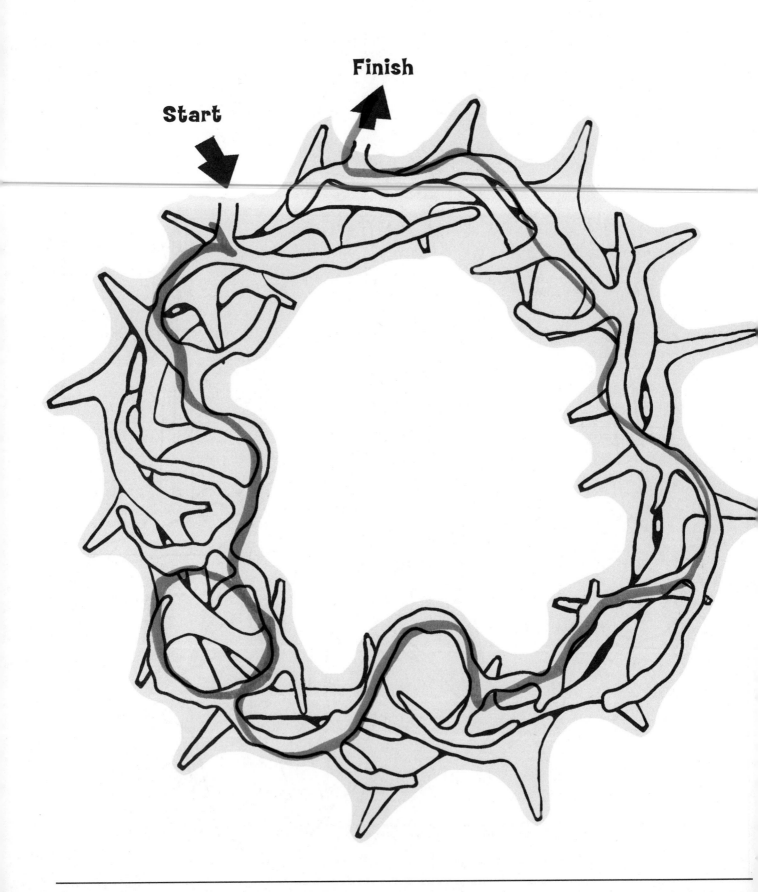

For God loved the world in this way: He gave his one and only Son, so that everyone who believes in him will not perish but have eternal life.

-John 3:16

Crossword: Crucifixion

Use the clues to write the answers from the word bank in the crossword puzzle below.

ACROSS
1. _____ Christ
2. Someone who saves us

DOWN
2. Things that don't please God
3. The opposite of dead
4. Jesus died because of His _____ for us

savior

alive

sins

Jesus

love

Find It: Resurrection Inspection

Find and circle all nine key words in the Bible story picture.

RESURRECTION TOMB DEATH BURIAL
SAVIOR JESUS CROSS EASTER ALIVE

Unscramble: Death and Resurrection

Unscramble the words to discover the message.

ESSUJ   DEID   NO   TEH

CORSS   OT   SVAE   PLEEOP

FOMR   ISN,   DAN

EH   SI   VALIE   YODAT

Maze: On the Road to Emmaus

Help the disciples get to Emmaus. Don't forget to meet Jesus on the way!

Jesus Appeared to the Disciples

Mark 16:14; Luke 24:36–43; John 20:19–29; Acts 1:3

Unscramble: Words of Jesus

Unscramble the words at the end to complete the sentences Jesus said to Peter.

"DO YOU _____ ME?"   VELO

"FEED MY _____."   PHSEE

" _____ ME!"   LOWOLF

Jesus Gave the Great Commission

Maze: Great Commission

Help the disciples get to Jesus.

Go, therefore, and make disciples of all nations, baptizing them in the name of the Father and of the Son and of the Holy Spirit, teaching them to observe everything I have commanded you. And remember, I am with you always, to the end of the age.

–Matthew 28:19-20

Secret Code: Great Commission

Cross out all the letters that are not in the words "Great Commission." Fill in the missing vowels using the key to find out what mission Jesus gave us.

GBHFRPUHEYBYAPYBT
CFBOMPYMUIFSYSBIOFN

CODE

A	(compass)
E	(heart)
I	(cross/book)
O	(hand)
U	(church)

What is our mission as believers?

_ _r   m_ss__h   _s

b_l___v_rs   _s   t_   m_k_

d_sc_pl_s   _f   _ll

n_t__ns   by   th_   p_w_r

_f   th_   Sp_r_t.

Jesus Ascended to Heaven

Maze: Ascension

Follow the cloud path to Jesus.

How Did Jesus Leave?

Jesus died and rose again. For 40 days, He talked with His disciples. Many other people saw Him too. Then He was taken into heaven. Circle the way you think He was taken to heaven. Color in the background.

Maze: Crucifixion and Resurrection

Complete the maze to show Jesus' journey from the cross to the grave and then to heaven.

The Holy Spirit Came

Peter Preached the Gospel

Acts 2:14–36

Hidden Message: Gospel

Color the spaces with dots yellow to find two words that describe the Gospel. Color the rest of the spaces different colors.

The Church Met Needs

Seven Men Were Chosen

Secret Code: What Is a Deacon?

The first deacons were chosen to help in the early church. Use the letter code to find another word for "deacon." Ex. B = Y

__ __ __ __ __ __ __
H   V   I   E   Z   M   G

Letter Code

A	B	C	D	E	F	G	H	I	J	K	L	M	N	O	P	Q	R	S	T	U	V	W	X	Y	Z
Z	Y	X	W	V	U	T	S	R	Q	P	O	N	M	L	K	J	I	H	G	F	E	D	C	B	A

Finish the Picture: Helping Hands

Draw two things in the hands below that you can do to help others.

Stephen's Address

Saul on the Road to Damascus

Acts 8:1–3; 9:1–31

Maze: Jesus Is Alive!

Complete the maze. Along the way, you'll pass through all the people who saw Jesus alive after He died on the cross.

Hidden Message: Word Puzzle

Find the answer to each math question. Color the puzzle pieces with the correct answers blue. Color the rest of the pieces any other color.

1. 1+4 = _____   2. 24-14 = _____   3. 5x3 = _____   4. 2+5+13 = _____

Look at the blue puzzle pieces. What new name did God give to Saul? _____

Paul's First Journey

Paul's Second Journey

Acts 15:36–16:40

Paul Preached in Europe

Maze: Paul's Journeys

Find the path that will take Paul from the large ship to the small boat that goes to shore. Don't get shipwrecked!

Paul's Third Journey

Church Responsibility

Find It: Letters to the Churches

Color in the circles with names of letters to the churches in the New Testament. Cross out the ones that are not names of letters.

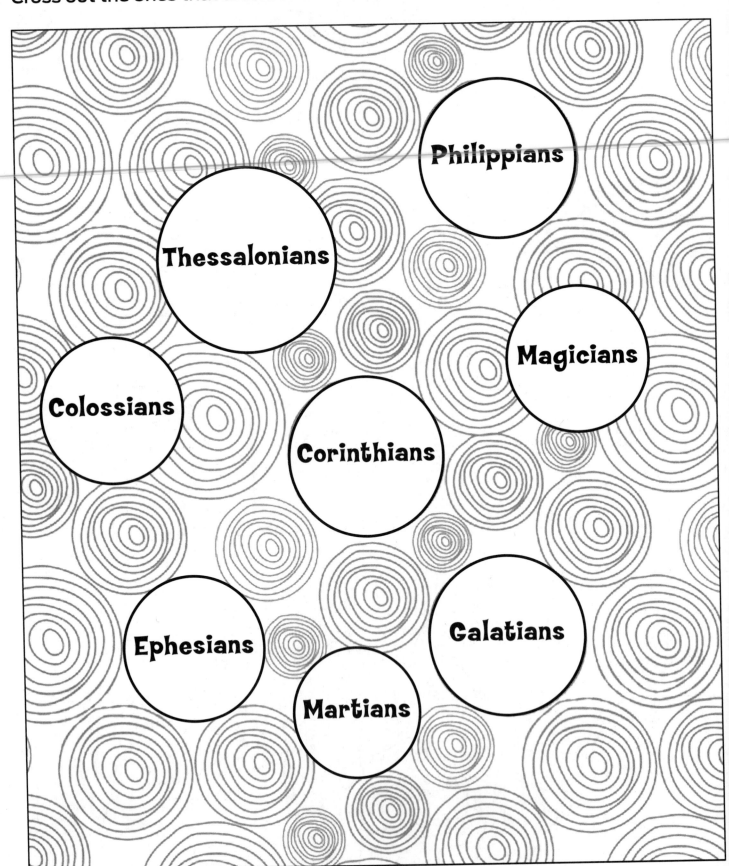

Philippians

Thessalonians

Magicians

Colossians

Corinthians

Ephesians

Galatians

Martians

Christ's Return Was Predicted

God's Warning to Seven Churches

Jesus Sits on the Throne

Find It: Matching Faces

Jesus came to save people from all nations, and people from all nations will be in heaven. Circle all of the faces that have a match.

Jesus Christ Will Return

Connect the Dots: Jesus

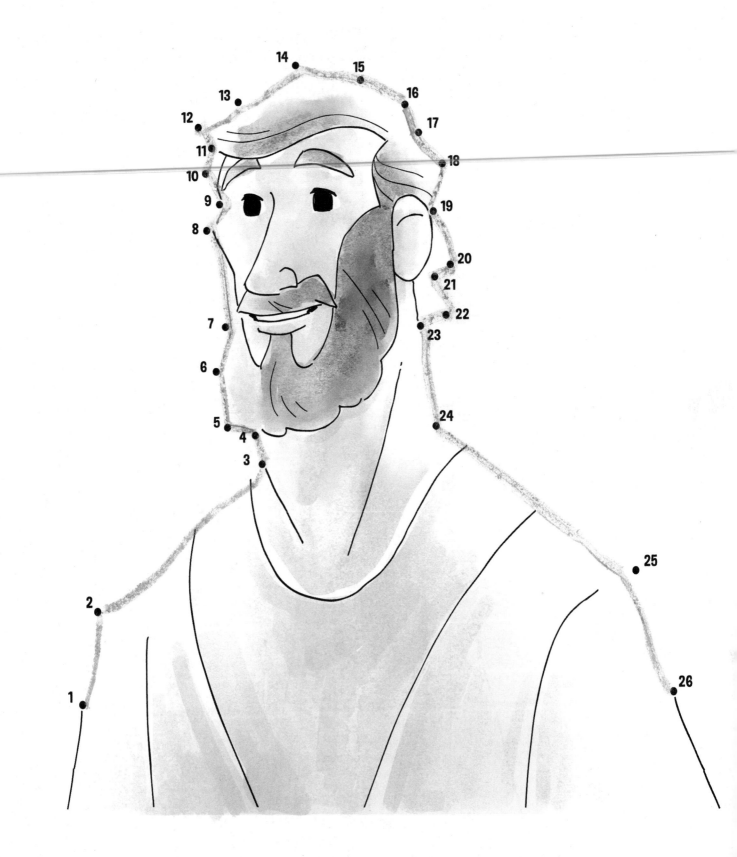

Heaven and earth will pass away, but my words will never pass away.
-Mark 13:31